25¢

Simple Sermons on the Old-time Religion

The "Simple Sermon" series by W. Herschel Ford . . .

Seven Simple Sermons on the Saviour's Last Words
Seven Simple Sermons on the Second Coming
Simple Sermons About Jesus Christ
Simple Sermons for a Sinful Age
Simple Sermons for Funeral Services
Simple Sermons for Midweek Services
Simple Sermons for Saints and Sinners
Simple Sermons for Special Days and Occasions
Simple Sermons for Sunday Evening
Simple Sermons for Sunday Morning
Simple Sermons for Time and Eternity
Simple Sermons for Times Like These
Simple Sermons for Today's World
Simple Sermons for 20th Century Christians
Simple Sermons on Conversion and Commitment
Simple Sermons From the Book of Acts
Simple Sermons From the Gospel of John
Simple Sermons From the Gospel of Matthew
Simple Sermons on Evangelistic Themes
Simple Sermons on Heaven, Hell and Judgment
Simple Sermons on Prayer
Simple Sermons on Prophetic Themes
Simple Sermons on Salvation and Service
Simple Sermons on Simple Themes
Simple Sermons on the Christian Life
Simple Sermons on Great Christian Doctrines
Simple Sermons on the Old-Time Religion
Simple Sermons on the Seven Churches of Revelation
Simple Sermons on the Ten Commandments
Simple Talks for Christian Workers
Simple Sermons on Life and Living
Simple Sermons for Modern Man
Simple Sermons on Old Testament Texts
Simple Sermons on New Testament Texts
Simple Sermons for a World in Crisis
Simple Sermons on Grace and Glory

Simple Sermons on the Old-time Religion

by
W. HERSCHEL FORD, D.D.

Introduction by Dr. W. A. Criswell

ZONDERVAN PUBLISHING HOUSE OF THE ZONDERVAN CORPORATION GRAND RAPIDS, MICHIGAN 49506

SIMPLE SERMONS ON THE OLD-TIME RELIGION
Copyright © 1968 by Zondervan Publishing House
Grand Rapids, Michigan

Tenth printing   1978
ISBN 0-310-24571-0

All rights reserved. No portion of this book may be reproduced
in any way without the written permission
of the publishers,
except for brief excerpts in magazine reviews, etc.

Library of Congress Catalog Card Number: 68-19842

Printed in the United States of America

DEDICATION
*This volume is affectionately
dedicated to*
Mr. Pat J. Zondervan
*great Christian gentleman,
dear friend,
my publisher for many years,
in love and appreciation.*

INTRODUCTION

Along with uncounted numbers of other preachers, I used to read these sermon books written by Dr. Herschel Ford and, along with my brethren, I was blessed and encouraged by them. It was my impression that more preachers read his books and preached his sermons than any other pulpiteer I knew. Since those early days, Dr. Ford has turned from the ministry of a pastor to that of an evangelist and, having moved to Dallas, now belongs to our beloved First Baptist Church. This has given me an even greater opportunity to know him and to see the fruit of his work. Needless to say, my love and appreciation for him and what he does has grown and grown with these passing days.

Of all the 25 volumes of the "Simple Sermon" series that Dr. Ford has published, none is more interesting or more "preachable" or more moving than this latest volume entitled *Simple Sermons on the Old-Time Religion*. These are sermons that preachers can preach, that teachers can teach, that students can study and that God's people can read with boundless profit. He delivers the message of God concerning the cardinal doctrines of the Christian faith. If a lost man reads them, he would most certainly be saved. God would speak to his heart through these sermons. Anyone who would open his mind and soul to these beautifully worded, magnificently outlined expositions of the truth of God will be gloriously blessed.

Possibly a left-wing liberal who has given up every vestige of belief in the Bible and in the old time religion would not rejoice in the sermons that Dr. Ford has published here, but the rest of us who love God, who have been washed in the blood of the Saviour and whose hearts are lifted up in the hope of Heaven, will praise God for the old-time faith the preacher here so marvelously presents. If you love Jesus and if you hope to see His face some day, you will love this book.

W. A. CRISWELL
Pastor, First Baptist Church
Dallas, Texas

AUTHOR'S FOREWORD

This is my twenty-fifth volume of "Simple Sermons." Never in my wildest imagination did I ever dream that I would author this many books when I wrote the first one. I am grateful to God for giving me this privilege and for the reception given these books by so many people.

I have a fourfold purpose in writing these books. First, to furnish preachers with sermonic suggestions and material. Second, to furnish help to Sunday school teachers and other Christian workers. Third, to point lost souls to the Saviour. Fourth, to edify and strengthen believers in Christ. I hope this present volume will do all four of these things.

Preachers and other Christian workers are invited and urged to use these messages as their very own.

W. Herschel Ford

CONTENTS

INTRODUCTION *by* W. A. Criswell

1. "Give Me That Old-Time Religion" JUDE 3 .. 13
2. The First Step Toward God LUKE 13:1-5 .. 22
3. "The Devil Will Get You if You Don't Watch Out" LUKE 22:31-34 .. 32
4. God's Favorite Word ISAIAH 1:18 .. 43
5. The Most Profitable Business in the World I TIMOTHY 4:8 .. 53
6. Sowing and Reaping GALATIANS 6:7 .. 62
7. The World's Worst Disease ROMANS 3:23 .. 70
8. When Life Really Begins JOHN 3:1-8 .. 78
9. "Revive Us Again" ISAIAH 1:1-18 .. 86
10. The Four-Square Gospel I COR 15:1-4 .. 95
11. "A Rendezvous With Death" HEBREWS 9:27-28 .. 105
12. The Message of the Empty Tomb LUKE 24:1-12 .. 113

1

"GIVE ME THAT OLD-TIME RELIGION"

Jude 3

There are three kinds of preachers in the world today. First, there is the modernist. He does not believe all of God's Word, he has no use for the cardinal doctrines of our faith and he despises the old-time religion. Then there is the "middle of the road" preacher. He tries to please everybody. To him everyone is good, no one is really lost. Then there is the preacher who is true to the Word. He knows men are lost and that Christ is their only hope.

There is a spiritual dearth in the land today. Millions are lost in sin. They completely ignore the church. God has no place in their lives. Other millions have their names on church rolls, yet their membership means nothing to them. I wonder how much of the blame for this condition can be laid at the doors of the preachers of our day. I speak of those who have failed to preach the "old-time religion," those who have gotten away from the true Gospel of Christ.

Jude admonishes us to "contend earnestly for the faith which was once delivered to the saints." The message is not a new message, but it is our only message. It is the same message which Peter proclaimed on the day of Pentecost, a message which turned 3,000 souls to Christ. It is the same message that Stephen proclaimed, the message which cut his hearers to the heart. It is the same message which Paul proclaimed before kings and jailers. He said, "I am not ashamed of the gospel of Christ: for it is the power of God unto salvation to every one that believeth" (Romans 1:16).

I. THE BASIC BELIEFS OF THE OLD-TIME RELIGION

1. *It includes the belief in a great God.* Today man looks at his own accomplishments and forgets the greatness of God. His slogan is, "Look what I did." God has allowed man to build skyscrapers, to make bombs that will destroy a nation, to fly around the world in a space ship in a few minutes' time. And man boasts of what he has done and God is left out.

But look at what GOD has done. He made the world and all that is in it. He made the sun, the moon, the stars, the milky way. He made the four seasons. He made night and day. He made all that man uses out of non-existent material. He created space. He made man, the most intricate piece of mechanism in the world. David said, "When I look at all Thy works, I wonder that You ever gave a thought to man."

Too many people today have a wrong conception of God. They think of Him as a big, beneficent Santa Claus. A certain man was drilling an oil well. He was eager to bring in a gusher. He was not ordinarily a praying man, but now he was desperate, so he prayed earnestly for success. The oil did come in and he looked up and said, "Thank You, Lord, You're a good scout." That's the way many people feel. They have no idea of the greatness and righteousness and holiness of God.

In a Gallup poll taken a few years ago it was found that 96% of Americans believed that there is a God, 1% did not believe He existed, and 3% were undecided. While many people believe in His existence, their God is too small. The old-time religion tells us of a great God, above and over all things, holy, righteous, almighty, a God whom we must someday face and to whom we must give an account of our lives.

2. *It includes the belief in the Lord Jesus Christ as the divine Saviour.* He was prophesied of old, He was born of a virgin, He lived a perfect life. He performed mighty miracles, He died on a cross. But He arose from the dead, He ascended into heaven, He intercedes for us daily and some-

day He is coming back. The old-time religion includes a belief in all of this and more.

There are some who call Jesus the "fairest flower of evolution." They call Him a "master teacher," the best man who ever lived. But He is much more than this. He is God incarnate. He is God uncovered. He is God come down to the world in human flesh.

But no one is saved by simply believing He was born and lived and died and rose and is coming again. The Bible tells the sinner that he must have a personal saving experience with Jesus Christ. The sinner must come to Him through repentance and faith. The only way to get to God is through Christ. He said, "No man cometh to the Father, but by me" (John 14:6). During the World War we heard men say, "I found God in a fox-hole." If they found Him there, it was because they came to Him through a personal experience with Christ. The life eternal that God gives must come through His Son. "Believe on the Lord Jesus Christ, and thou shalt be saved" (Acts 16:31).

3. *It includes the belief in the Holy Spirit, the third Person of the Trinity.* The Holy Spirit is simply God working in the human heart. Someone has said that God could not be everywhere, therefore He made mothers. They are wrong. God is everywhere in the person of the Holy Spirit. He comes first to convict us of sin and point us to the Saviour. Then He abides in the heart forever, to guide, to comfort, to teach. The old-time religion recognizes and honors the Holy Spirit as the third Person of the Godhead.

4. *It includes the belief in the Bible as God's Word to man.* We read in II Peter 1:21 that "holy men of God spake as they were moved by the Holy Ghost." These were the men who wrote the Bible. They used their hands, but God was speaking through those hands. The Bible was written by 40 men over a period of 1,500 years and the one book contains 66 books. But every part fits perfectly into every other part.

The Bible and the Bible alone is our guide to faith and practice. When someone asks, "What is your creed?" we can say, "Here it is, the Bible itself is our creed. We believe it from the Creation in Genesis to the last 'Amen' in Revelation."

5. *It includes the belief that salvation comes only through Christ.* When we come in faith to Him, He forgives our sin, He saves us, He regenerates us. He writes our names down in the Lamb's Book of Life and preserves us unto the perfect day.

A prominent preacher some years ago said that "the blood of Jesus Christ has no more power than the blood of a chicken." But the Bible says that "the blood of Jesus Christ his Son cleanses us from all sin" (I John 1:7). So we sing

> There is a fountain filled with blood,
> Drawn from Immanuel's veins,
> And sinners plunged beneath that flood,
> Lose all their guilty stains.

and

> What can wash away my sin?
> Nothing but the blood of Jesus.
> What can make me whole again?
> Nothing but the blood of Jesus.

Your good life cannot save you. Your good deeds and your gifts cannot save you. Your church membership cannot save you. You say, "I have never harmed anyone." You can't base your salvation on that assumption, for you have trampled under foot the One who died for you. I heard someone say about a soldier, "He died for his country, so surely he will be received into heaven." No, it is not a case of your dying for someone, it is a case of putting your faith in Someone who died for you.

6. *It includes the belief in a life that never ends.* The Gallup poll showed that 76% of all Americans believed in a future life, 13% did not believe in it, and 11% had no opinion about it. Oh, that men would believe God and His Word and not go by their own opinions and fancies! Daniel said, "And many of them that sleep in the dust of the earth shall awake, some to everlasting life, and some to shame and everlasting contempt" (12:2).

There are two sides to immortality, eternal life and eternal death. You make the choice. Life and heaven are yours in Christ. Death and hell are yours if you reject Him.

7. *It includes the belief in heaven and hell.* Heaven is where Jesus will be. It is a place of reunion with our loved ones, a place of perfect happiness and joy. Hell is where the devil is, a place of suffering and separation and sorrow. We have too much soft preaching today. Hell is never mentioned in many pulpits. But the Bible teaching on this subject is clear and plain and must not be ignored. Yes, God is a God of love and mercy, but He is also a just God, a God of judgment and wrath.

II. The Blessed Benefits of the Old-time Religion

1. *It will bring forgiveness of sin.* There is a black record of our sin against God. The only way to receive forgiveness is in the Christ of the old-time religion. Do you remember the "Wordless Book" which soul-winners often use to explain salvation? The first page is black, representing our sin. The second page is red, representing the blood of Christ which covers our sin when we come to Him. The third page is white, picturing the soul washed white in the blood of the Lamb. The fourth page is gold, symbolizing heaven. That black page remains black until Christ enters the heart.

2. *It will bring us into right relationship with God.* Before we come to Christ we are at enmity with God, we are not God's children. Men talk glibly today about "the Fatherhood of God." But in a redemptive sense we are not the children of God. In our natural state, we are the chlldren of Satan. "Ye are of your father the devil, and the lusts of your father ye will do" (John 8:44).

John 1:12 clearly shows that before we come to Christ we are not God's children. Only those who receive Him as Saviour become the children of God. "But as many as received him, to them gave he power to become the sons of God, even to them that believe on his name."

Before I met Christ I tried to pray each night. I thought that I ought to do this. But prayer meant nothing to me until I could really call God "Father" after I became His child.

3. *It will change your life.* "Therefore if any man be in Christ, he is a new creature: old things are passed away; behold, all things are become new" (II Corinthians 5:17).

Let me share a letter I received sometime ago from a man in my radio congregation:

> Happy am I that I turned my radio on in time to hear your broadcast this morning for it turned me around. It gave me just the nudge I needed to turn again into the fold, for I am a "has been" that you so vividly pictured this morning. So tonight I am going back into the church. I am now discarding a habit that has kept me away for several months. I have been saying after this week I shall stop and it has been this way all along — for each consecutive week the possibilities of this speculation has appeared more and more promising. And now I am through. I used to sing in the choir and teach a Sunday school class, but today I am only a "has been." Tonight I am going back home. I am sure you can now see how effective your broadcasts are. I cannot promise to listen again for I plan now to be in church every Sunday morning from now on. May God ever bless you and renew and strengthen your courage and power to preach the truth to a weak generation.

Why did this man change? Why did he turn back to God and the church? It was because he took the Gospel and applied it to his own heart and life. If you will let the Gospel of the old-time religion have its way with you, it will change you, also.

4. *It will give you a daily companion.* Some years ago a popular song had the title, "I'll Walk Alone." The Christian never has to say that. He will always have a sweet and wonderful Companion. Sorrows may come, tears may fall, life may be difficult, the heart may ache, but always we can hear that Companion saying, "Fear not, I am with thee. I'll make all things work together for your good. I'll never let anything come your way that you and I cannot handle together."

5. *It will give you the privilege of prayer.* There is only one prayer for the sinner to pray. His prayer is, "God be

merciful to me, a sinner." But after he is saved he can claim a score of prayer promises. Jesus said, "And whatsoever ye shall ask in my name, that will I do, that the Father may be glorified in the Son" (John 14:13).

Does that mean that you can have anything you want? Does that mean that God will give you a Cadillac or a new home or a million dollars if you simply ask Him for these things? No, for when we ask in His name and according to His will and that God might be glorified, that does away with foolish requests.

Often a Christian makes some enemies. They try to hurt him by using all kinds of weapons, gossip, lies, trickery, accusations. Now the Christian cannot use these weapons in return. He must not. His only weapon is prayer. If we live rightly, abiding in God's Word and praying, we need not fear what any man can do to us.

6. *It gives you hope for the future.* The sinner boasts and says, "I am not afraid of the future." Yet he has nothing on which to base his confidence. But the Christian can say, "I have hope for the future." His hope is based on "nothing less than Jesus' blood and righteousness." Oh, what a difference!

During the war our navy advertised for anchors weighing five thousand pounds or more. I don't know how many they found, but I do know that the Christian has found an anchor in Christ and that his future is as bright as the morning star.

7. *It gives you help in the hour of death.* The Psalmist said, "Yea, though I walk through the valley of the shadow of death, I will fear no evil: for thou art with me" (Psalm 23:4). What a blessed assurance! One day when the last task has been completed, when the last song has been sung and the last tear has been shed, our feet shall touch the icy waters of the river of death, but, thank God, we shall not be alone. We shall feel His hand upon us, guiding us toward the everlasting sunlight and the mansions of glory. It's enough to make us shout "Hallelujah!"

When our two boys were little, they would often go to sleep in the car. When we reached home I would gently put them in their little beds and when they waked up in the morning they would find themselves safe at home. That's what death means to a Christian. We go to sleep in the arms of Jesus and wake up in glory.

8. *It gives you entrance into heaven.* There are two ways in which a Christian might enter heaven. He may go through the avenue of death or he may go up when Jesus returns in the air. If you are trusting Him you are safe, whether you die or are living when He comes.

On a recent Christmas day a man walked through a Toronto hospital, giving away one-hundred dollar bills. Any of us would like to meet that man. But, oh, it will mean so much more to meet Jesus! He will not give us hundred-dollar bills, but He will give us heaven and all that it holds. That's the old-time religion — "All this and heaven, too."

III. How Can You Get the Old-time Religion

That's an easy question. Just get Christ and you'll have it. You come to Him through repentance and faith. "Except ye repent, ye shall all likewise perish" (Luke 13:3). Repentance will bring you to a personal acceptance of Christ as Saviour and Lord. "Behold, I stand at the door and knock: if any man hear my voice, and open the door, I will come in to him, and will sup with him, and he with me" (Revelation 3:20).

Then repentance and faith are followed by an open confession of Christ. "For with the heart man believeth unto righteousness; and with the mouth confession is made unto salvation" (Romans 10:10).

After this initial experience with Him, which the old-timers called "getting religion," will come obedience, baptism, church membership, giving, Christian living and serving.

A preacher conducted a revival near the campus of a great university. One night a well-dressed young man came into the church. The pastor whispered to the visiting preacher, "That young man has the keenest intellect of any student in the university. His grandfather erected a building on the campus. He was a great Christian, but the boy is an avowed atheist." The sermon that night was on the subject, "How may we know that there is a God?"

"Give Me That Old-time Religion"

The next afternoon the young man sought out the visiting preacher to ask him some questions. They sat in the pastor's study and talked throughout the time for the evening meal. At 8 o'clock the service began. They could hear the songs in the church but they kept on talking. Soon the preacher said, "I must go to the pulpit now, but I would like to ask you a question. Have I been honest with you?" The young man replied, "You surely have." "Well then," said the preacher, "won't you be just as honest? Won't you turn away from your skepticism and trust your father's and mother's Saviour? If so give me your hand."

The young man started to give the preacher his hand, but instead he threw his arms around him and sobbed out his repentance on the preacher's shoulder. That night in the church he made his full surrender to the Lord Jesus Christ. The next day he said to the preacher, "Mother and father are gone but I wish I could wire them and tell them what has happened. But I'll see them in heaven one day and won't they be surprised to see me?"

One year later the brilliant young man died and went home to be with his loved ones and his Lord. Thank God for the old-time religion. Don't you want it?

2

THE FIRST STEP TOWARD GOD

Luke 13:1-5

In this age of religious confusion we often hear the questions, "How can I get through to God? I need help and strength and wisdom. How can I get to the source of help and strength and wisdom? How can I get through to God?" Now a Russian astronaut went up into space several years ago and when he returned he made a startling declaration. He said, "I looked everywhere up there for God and I couldn't find Him. Therefore I declare to you that there is no God." The Psalmist was thinking of him when he said, "The fool hath said in his heart, There is no God" (Psalm 14:1).

But God is out there and God is down here. The Eternal God is everywhere. He is big enough to fill all of the universe, but He is small enough to live in your heart and mine. He is "closer than hands and feet and nearer than breathing." And those who seek God can find Him. "When you seek Me with all your heart, I will be found of you," God says (Jeremiah 29:13, 14).

Men try to find God in different ways. The savage tries to find God by inflicting punishment upon himself. He cuts his body and brings out the blood, hoping that some god, somewhere, will see that blood and look with favor upon him. The pagan seeks God in another way. He bows down before idols of wood or stone or metal and worships an inanimate object.

When I was in Japan on a preaching mission I went down to the little village of Kamakura to see the "Big Buddha."

The First Step Toward God

This statue of the pagan god sits on a mound of earth in a beautiful little park. The statue is about as high as a five story building and has been sitting there for 700 years. On the day I was there a tray of tangerines had been set before Buddha. I was told that each morning some fruit or food or flowers were put there for him to enjoy.

I learned that you could go up on the inside of the statue for ten yen, so I bought my ticket, went inside and climbed a ladder almost up to the statue's head. I found that Buddha was nothing but a hollow metal shell. I saw no heart, no brain, nothing. So that night, when I went back and preached to my Japanese congregation, I told them about my experience. I said, "Today I went up on the inside of the Big Buddha. I saw no brain, with which he might think for you. I saw no heart, with which he might love you. I saw only a hollow metal statue that has been sitting there for 700 years, doing nothing for anybody. Now let me tell you about my God, the God of heaven, who is alive, who knows all about you, who loves you so much that He gave His Son to die for you."

Yes, men seek God in various ways. The civilized man seeks Him in forms and rituals. He goes through these forms week after week until he knows all the ritual by heart. But he doesn't find God in his formal, ritualistic religion. He goes to church, goes through all the man-made ceremony, yet comes away with a hungry heart, because he has had no intimate touch with Christ. He is not to be found in forms and religious rites.

There is just one way to find God and that is the Bible way. It is the way of repentance and faith, repentance toward God and faith in the Lord Jesus Christ. Jesus said, "No man cometh unto the Father but by me" (John 14:6). So I want to talk to you about repentance, the first step to God. No man reaches God until he takes this step.

Now I do not preach repentance apart from faith. They are twin doctrines, they are inseparable graces. If a man really and truly repents of his sin he will exercise faith in

Christ. If he exercises saving faith in Christ, it is evident that he has first repented of his sin.

Jesus had excuse-makers around in His day, just as we have today. As He preached about forsaking sin and eternal life and salvation, someone said, "What about those Galileans who were killed by Pilate? Didn't it happen because they were such sinners?" But Jesus brought them right back to the subject. He said, "You have no right to judge them, but unless you repent you will perish." Then someone else said, "What about those eighteen who were killed when the tower in Siloam fell upon them? They must have been the worst sinners in Jerusalem." But Jesus replied, "What happened to them doesn't affect you. The issue is between you and God and unless you repent you will perish." (See Luke 13:1-5.) And so men make all kinds of excuses today for not following Christ. But regardless of others and what they do, the cardinal fact still remains that if men will not repent, they will surely perish.

Repentance is the first step to God. God and heaven and eternal life can never be yours until you have first repented of your sins.

I. Repentance Is a Great Biblical Doctrine

The prophets of the Old Testament went up and down the land, calling upon the people to repent of their sin and turn to God. John the Baptist, preaching to the multitudes who flocked to hear him, preached, "Repent . . . for the kingdom of heaven is at hand" (Matthew 3:2). In our text Jesus was telling men to repent or perish. On the day of Pentecost Peter called upon the people to repent and three thousand responded in a day. The great apostle, Paul, preached that salvation came from "repentance toward God, and faith toward our Lord Jesus Christ" (Acts 20:21). And every great gospel preacher down over the ages has sounded out the truth that God "commandeth all men every where to repent" (Acts 17:30).

But the doctrine of repentance is not pleasant to the natural man, for it includes the forsaking of sin. And when you talk to a man about giving up a sin that is dear to his heart, he rebels against it. He doesn't want to hear about it. He will give up anything before giving up his sin.

Sometime ago I asked a man the question, "How do you like your new pastor?" He replied, "I like him quite well, but some of our members don't like him because he preaches too pointedly about their pet sins." There it is. This is a repulsive doctrine to many. They want to hear about the love of God, the grace of Christ, the joys of the Christian life, the glories of heaven. But they don't want to hear about their sins and repentance.

II. WHAT REPENTANCE IS NOT

1. *It is not the fear of God.* Some men, on what they fear is their deathbed, cry out to God for forgiveness. Then, when they recover, they go right back to their old sin. This is not true repentance, this is simply the fear of God.

One night in Dallas, when Dr. Truett was about to close out the prayer meeting service in the First Baptist Church on Wednesday night, a doctor entered the auditorium and said, "Just a minute, pastor, I have a request to make. Down the street there is a man who is critically ill. I don't believe he has long to live. He asked me if this were not the night when the people gathered together for prayer. When I answered that it was, he asked me to ask you to pray for him. He wants you to tell God that if He will let him recover, he will come to church, accept Christ as his Saviour, and live a Christian life. Pastor, will you pray and make that promise to God for him?" And the great preacher prayed an earnest prayer, pleading for the man and making his promise to God.

The next day the doctor found the man greatly improved. In a few days he was out of bed, in a few more days he was back at work. Then on a Saturday the pastor met him on the street. He said to the man, "You'll be in church tomorrow, won't you?" And the man replied, "I'm sorry, but I can't come. I got behind in my work while I was sick and I must work tomorrow." "But," said the preacher, "don't you remember the promise you made to God?" "Oh, yes," said the man, "I was desperate then and I had to do something. But one day I'll come and carry out my promise." The days went by and the man didn't come to church. Then one morning the pastor read in the paper that the man had been standing at a railroad station the day before, talking and laughing with some other men. Suddenly he clapped his hand to his side and fell upon the pavement, dead. The preacher said that for many days the only Scripture he could think of was, "To day if ye will hear his voice, harden not your hearts" (Hebrews 4:7). The fear of God is not repentance.

2. *Repentance is not simply sorrow for sin.* You can weep rivers of tears, you can clothe yourself in sackcloth and ashes, yet a simple feeling of sorrow over sin is not all of repentance.

3. *Repentance is not merely conviction for sin.* Many people go to church and come under deep conviction. The Holy Spirit convicts them through a sermon or a song. But they do nothing about it and repentance does not follow.

My first pastorate was in a little church on the edge of Atlanta, Georgia. Every Sunday night a man would come out from the city, have supper with some of his relatives, and come to church with them. One Sunday night I took this man into a small Sunday school room and talked to him about giving his heart to Christ. He told me the following story. "Several years ago I went to a revival meeting every night. I came under deep conviction for sin. I could hardly sleep by night or eat by day. But I did nothing about it. I let the meeting close without turning from my sin to the Lord. Since that time I have had no feeling, no desire, no impulse to come to the Lord. My heart has been like stone about spiritual matters over the years since then. I have crossed over the line." I pled with that man. I told him that God offered free salvation to every man, for He said, "Whosoever will, let him come." I prayed with him, I quoted Scripture to him, but all in vain. He had been convicted but conviction is not enough.

4. *Repentance is not merely a profession of Christ with the lips.* It goes down deeper than that and changes the whole life and heart. In other days I lived near a man who

The First Step Toward God

had no use for the church or spiritual things. Seemingly he lived a godless life. He died very suddenly one day, and I was called on to conduct his funeral. Just before the funeral service a man came to me and said, "That man was my brother. I wanted you to know that he made a profession of religion twenty-five years ago in a lumber camp." Of course he expected me to picture the man going right through the gates of glory.

But a mere profession of religion which does not include a turning away from sin and trusting the Saviour is not repentance.

5. *Repentance is not merely being baptized and joining the church.* It is more than a religious form. Nicodemus was religious, but Jesus told him that it was necessary for him to be born again. Repentance is not being whitewashed in baptism, but being washed white in the blood of the Lamb.

III. WHAT, THEN, IS REPENTANCE?

1. *It is a complete change of heart and life.* It is a turning from sin to the Saviour. It is coming over on God's side and taking His side against sin. Here is a man in the army. He receives the command to march and he marches forward. Then the command "halt" is given. He halts and the command "about face and forward march" is given. He makes two movements as he turns about. In these two movements we see the drama of conversion.

An unsaved man is marching toward sin and Satan and hell. His back is toward God and Christ and the church and eternal life. Then the Captain of his soul cries out, "About face and forward march." He takes two steps, the step of repentance and the step of faith. He marches forward in a new life. Now his back is toward sin and Satan and hell. He is facing God, walking with Christ, serving in the church and headed toward heaven. That is a simple picture of repentance coupled with faith.

2. *It is a continuing change of heart and life.* Repentance unto salvation is a one-time thing. But since we sin daily, there needs to be a continuous spirit of repentance on our

part. The correct translation of 1 John 3:9 is "whosoever is born of God doth not continue in his old sin." He will not make a practice of sin as he did in the days before his conversion, but he will surely sin from time to time through his old carnal nature.

Therefore the Christian will daily come to God in confession of sin and repentance. He realizes that every sin is a slap in the face of Almighty God, every sin grieves the Holy Spirit. He will always want to make things right with God by his daily repentance. And as he more and more practices repentance, he will sin less and less.

So we see that primarily salvation comes through repentance and faith, by turning from sin to the Saviour. Then, secondly, cleansing comes through a life of constant turning to God in confession and repentance.

IV. WHAT DOES REPENTANCE DO FOR A PERSON?

1. *Repentance brings him into right relationship to Jesus.* He says to his sin, "Good-by, sin, I am going with Jesus. From now on I am through with you." A man who never gives up his sin can never know Jesus.

Dr. Robert Stuart McArthur served for many years as pastor of the Calvary Baptist Church of New York City. One Sunday night a very wealthy man said to him, "Dr. McArthur, you know I am rich. If I come to Christ, would I have to give up my wealth?" Dr. McArthur replied, "I do not know. That would be between you and God." Then the man said, "Well, I am going to consider this matter seriously for one week. I'll give you my decision next Sunday night." The man's sin must have been his love for money, for the next Sunday night he said to Dr. McArthur, "Dr. McArthur, I have decided to hold on to my money, and if God and Christ and heaven must go, I'll simply let them go."

Yes, if a man will not come to God in repentance and faith, he gives up all that Christ can mean to him on this earth and he gives up eternal life.

2. *Repentance brings him into a local church.* If a man

tells me that he has been converted, yet he refuses to join a church, I have some doubts as to the genuineness of his conversion. When a man has had the tremendous experience of the new birth, surely he will want to follow the Saviour into a fellowship of believers. Christ founded the church and put it on earth for a purpose. It is the only divinely instituted organization in the world. Christ placed the church here for men to live in and serve through. You can have some doubt of your salvation if you say, "I have been saved, but I am not going to join a local church."

3. *Repentance causes him to straighten up the past.* When the Philippian jailer found Christ as his Saviour, his first act was to wash the stripes of Paul and Silas. Earlier in the evening he had taken keen delight in beating those poor preachers, but now that he had been saved he tenderly ministered to them. Do you need to do any stripe-washing? Are there some things in your past that you ought to make right? If you have repented of your sins, you ought to go back and straighten up the past as far as it is possible to do so.

One night at the close of a service a little girl came up to Gypsy Smith and handed him a fountain pen. She was weeping as she did it. "Why do you give me this pen?" asked the great evangelist. And the little girl explained, "I stole it from my little friend. She thinks that she lost it. After hearing your sermon tonight I feel that I want to be a Christian, but this fountain pen stands between me and Christ." Mr. Smith told her to take the pen back to the other little girl, confessing the theft and telling her how she felt. The girl agreed to do this. The next night she came forward to give her heart to Christ when the invitation was given. Right behind her came the girl from whom she had stolen the fountain pen. She had been so impressed by the first girl's testimony and action that she felt her need of the Saviour, also.

Maybe if some of us would go back and pay off some old debts, settle some old quarrels, do some apologizing and straightening out of the past, then more people would have some confidence in our religion.

4. *Repentance causes rejoicing.* It will cause rejoicing in heaven. The Bible tells us that there is joy in heaven over even one sinner who repents. This joy is in the hearts of the angels, it may be in the hearts of our loved ones who are there, and surely there is joy in the heart of Jesus.

Then there is joy in our own hearts. There is no such joy anywhere as the joy that comes to a new-born child of God. Then there is joy in the hearts of others. Those who love us and pray for us rejoice when we come to the Lord in a genuine conversion experience.

Yes, repentance is the first step to God. The Chinese proverb tells us that "a journey of a thousand miles begins with a single step." Why not take that step right now? If you'll do it, you will find Jesus waiting for you, ready to adopt you into the family of God, ready to forgive all your sins, ready to walk down life's pathway with you and take you to heaven at the end of the way.

General John B. Gordon, the famous Confederate leader, was a candidate for the United States Senate from Georgia. In those days they elected their senators, not by popular vote, but by the vote of the State Legislature. In one Georgia county the political leaders did not like General Gordon, so they elected their legislator on the platform and pledge that he would go to the state capitol and vote against General Gordon. The day came for the election and General Gordon was elected as the United States Senator from Georgia. The next morning, when the people in that particular county read about General Gordon's election, they learned that their representative had voted for the general and helped to elect him.

They sent for him to come home and upon his return they had an indignation mass meeting. They said to him, "Why did you betray our trust? We sent you to the legislature to vote against General Gordon, yet you voted for him and helped to elect him. Why did you do it?" And he replied, "I did not mean to betray your trust but, you see, I had never seen General Gordon. Then one day as I stood in the Senate chamber talking to another legislator, the door opened and a striking looking man came in. I noticed that he had a livid scar on his face, running from his temple down to his jaw. So I said to my friend, 'Who is that unusual looking man with that awful scar on his face?' And he answered, 'Why that is General John B. Gordon, candidate for the United States Senate.' No my friends, I did not mean to betray your trust, but when I saw that awful scar on the general's face and knew he received it as he fought for you and me, I just couldn't find it in my heart to vote against him."

Oh, I wish I could show you another One today, the Saviour who bears the scars He received as He suffered and died for you and me. And I would say to you, "As you come to realize what He did for you and what He wants to do for you, how can you find it in your heart to vote against Him?"

Won't you then, repent of your sin and put all your trust in Him? Remember that for you it is repent or perish, turn or burn, life or death, heaven or hell. Which will it be?

3

"THE DEVIL WILL GET YOU IF YOU DON'T WATCH OUT"

Luke 22:31-34

I take you today to an upper room in the city of Jerusalem. Several men are sitting around a table. They have just finished their meal. Their faces are filled with sadness. Their Leader, who sits in the center, has just told them that He is soon to die, that He is going to be crucified. But even though He was facing death, His thoughts were not of Himself, but of others. He tried to comfort His friends by saying, "Let not your heart be troubled, you believe in God, believe also in Me. I am going away to prepare a place where you will be with me forever."

Then His eyes lighted on Peter, the most outstanding of all His disciples. Peter was no ordinary man, he was far above the average. He rose higher and sank lower than any of Christ's disciples. Now Jesus knew this big impulsive man would be sorely tested, so He said to him, "Peter, Satan is going to tempt you, but I will be praying for you." The testing time soon came and Peter went down miserably. But all the time Jesus was praying for him. And His prayers were answered. Peter repented of his sins, and wept his heart out in bitter sorrow. He came back to be the great preacher of Pentecost and finally to die a martyr's death.

Just as the devil got hold of Peter and sifted him as wheat, causing the world to see the chaff in his life, so does he want to get hold of you and me. If you are redeemed, he knows he can't keep you out of heaven. But he wants you to sin and thus lose your witness and influence. He wants to be

The Devil Will Get You If You Don't Watch Out

able to point you out to someone else and say, "Look at him. He is a Christian, but look at the sin and anger and rebellion and jealousy and lust and selfishness in his life." Thus he ruins our influence.

I. THERE IS A DEVIL

The Bible tells us that he was once in heaven, an angel of great power, intelligence and beauty. Then he rebelled against God and God hurled him out of heaven. Since that time he and the angels who fell with him have been fighting God and His work. He is a mighty being but not almighty. He is entirely evil himself and heads up all the evil in the world. He is behind everything bad that exists today.

The Bible tells us that he exists and Jesus spoke of him and spoke to him. Peter, John and Paul spoke of him. The Bible tells us of his various appearances on earth. Our own experience attests to the fact that he exists. We don't go far down life's pathway until we meet him. He tempts us, he goads us to evil, he does everything imaginable to tear us down.

Many modern men scoff at the idea of a personal devil. They say he is simply the "figment of a distorted imagination." I would like to ask you this question — if there is no devil, if there is no master-mind of evil in the world, who is doing the devil's work today? Who is behind every bloody war that snuffs out the lives of our sons? Who is behind all the cheap political intrigue? Who is behind the greed and graft in high places? Who is behind all the lust and sin and selfishness that drags men down? Who is behind all the jealousy and envy and ill-feeling and hatred in men's hearts? The answer is simple. His name is Satan, the devil, that old serpent.

Is the devil real? Ask Eve who listened to him and lost all she had, who was driven from the fairest home any human ever lived in. Ask Job. The devil put him to the test and he, too, lost all — his family, his property, his health. Yes, he lost all but God. Ask Jesus. He battled him in the wilderness and defeated him with the Word of God. Ask every man who has tried to live for God and they will tell you of their battles with Satan. Our prisons are full of people today who fought Satan and lost. But heaven and earth are teeming with the multitudes who fought him and won over him in the strength of the Almighty.

You can't do business with the devil and prosper. You can't appease him. Neville Chamberlain of England tried to appease Hitler and it didn't work. The world was plunged into a bloody war. And every attempt at appeasement or compromise with Satan brings us to disaster and defeat. He must be overcome in the power of the Spirit.

II. THE DEVIL WANTS EVERY SOUL

He knows the work of Christ. He knows how the Saviour can save a man and make him over and make him a credit to God. So he does all he can to avert this. His big job is to tear down the work of the Saviour.

We are told in the Old Testament how he tried to ruin one of God's best men. God said to him, "Have you seen Job, have you noticed how he serves me?" And Satan answered, "But you have him hedged about with every good thing. Let me at him. Let me take some of these things away and he will curse you to your face." God permitted Satan to bring sorrow and loss to Job, but Job remained loyal to God. In the New Testament we see him going after Peter, seeking to ruin him, the chief disciple. He didn't go after Judas. He had him already, but he went after a higher mark. Always he tries to hurt God's man.

A man may say, "He never tempts me." Maybe it's because he already has you in his clutches and he doesn't have to worry about you. He knows you will serve him. But another says, "I am having a fierce battle. I want to be the best Christian possible, but Satan faces me and fights me on every side." That man recognizes that he has an adversary. There is hope for him.

III. WHAT DOES THE DEVIL WANT YOU TO DO?

1. *He wants you to drift away from the Church.* When you were first saved and joined the church, you attended

The Devil Will Get You If You Don't Watch Out

every service. You could hardly wait from one service to the next. Then something came up and you quit the prayer meeting. Satan laughed, "Ha, ha, I have him now." Soon you missed church on Sunday night and soon you were not even attending on Sunday morning. Finally the devil said, "I won't have to worry about him any more. He has lost his influence for Christ." There are thousands of Christians like this. They never go to God's house, they give nothing, they can't witness for Christ. Their Christian testimony has been nullified.

What happens when we drift away from the church? (1) We disobey God's command, which says that we are not to forsake "the assembling of ourselves together" (Hebrews 10:25). He put the church here for us to live in and serve through. (2) We disobey His command about the Lord's Supper. He said, "This do oft in remembrance of me." When we fail to attend church, we fail to obey this injunction. (3) We disobey His command to give our tithes and offerings. Those who never come, never give. (4) We disobey His command to witness. You don't have a witness if you aren't faithful to the church. (5) You bring reproach upon the cause of Christ. Your very example says, "There is nothing to Christianity." (6) You starve your own soul, your spiritual life. The very least a Christian can do is to attend the services of his church. But the devil is glad when he can get you to drift.

2. *He wants you to take it easy.* "Woe to them that are at ease in Zion" (Amos 6:1). Christianity is a militant religion. It is not a soft bed to lie on until God takes you to heaven. It's a struggle all the way. Paul tells us to "fight the good fight" (I Timothy 6:12). He is telling us that the Christian life is no bed of roses. Sin and self clamor for the upper hand. And when a Christian gives way to the desire for ease, he immediately loses the battle.

It is easier to stay in bed on Sunday morning than to get up and go to church. It is easier to give in to the flesh than to say, "No." It is easier to rest than to resist. It is easier to sleep than to struggle. If the devil can get you to take it easy, he laughs with glee. He catches you off guard, causes you to sin, and wins the victory.

3. *He wants you to neglect the Bible.* You buy a Bible, read it faithfully for a while, then lay it aside. People often bring their Bible to church, leave them there and never call for them. The devil knows if you store God's Word in your heart you can defeat him, so he persuades you to neglect it. The Psalmist said, "Thy word have I hid in mine heart, that I might not sin against thee" (Psalm 119:11). His word must be hidden in the heart, and not left on the table.

An agnostic and a preacher sat at the same table in a railway dining car, and both of them ordered fish, which was very palatable and enjoyable. The agnostic said to the preacher, "Do you preach the Bible?" "Oh yes," replied the preacher. "You don't understand it all, do you?" "No," answered the preacher. "Well," said the agnostic, "what do you do about that?" The preacher said, "Just as I do in eating this delicious fish. When I come to the bone I lay it on one side of my plate and go on enjoying the fish. If some fool insists on choking to death on the bones, that's his misfortune."

No, we don't understand all of the Bible. But we can understand enough to feed our souls on the finest spiritual food. Don't let the devil divorce you from the Bible.

4. *He wants you to neglect your prayer life.* The old couplet says,

> Satan trembles when he sees
> The weakest saint upon his knees.

Would a soldier go to meet the enemy unarmed? Of course not. He arms himself with the most modern equipment. Yet we often go to fight the world, the flesh and the devil and lay aside our mightiest weapon, prayer.

It is mighty hard for the devil to defeat a praying man or a praying church. When we witness great victories in our church we know that they did not come from our words or our work. They came because of prayer. When we rely upon organization we get what organization can do. When

The Devil Will Get You If You Don't Watch Out 37

we rely upon education we get what education can do. When we rely upon eloquence we get what eloquence can do. But when we rely upon prayer we get what God can do.

Some years ago my wife and I took a steamship trip up the coast of Alaska. I was asked to preach on the ship on Sunday morning. On this particular morning the fog was very heavy, so it was necessary to blow the ship's fog-horn every thirty seconds. Of course I could not compete with that horn. But some of us began to pray for the fog to lift. The service was to begin at 10:30 o'clock. At 10:25 the fog lifted, the fog-horn was silenced and I was able to preach. It was a good service. A young couple from California came under conviction in that service. Later I was able to witness to them in their cabin and they gave their hearts to Jesus. Prayer was the power behind it all.

But Satan causes us to neglect prayer. He knows that in this way he can rob the Christian of his greatest help and strength.

5. *He wants you to lower your standards.* Christianity presents the highest standard of living. The devil loves to see us lower these standards. When a man holds up the banner of a good life, when he lives according to the highest standards, the world says, "Ah, there's a real Christian." But when a Christian lowers his standards, all the world says, "There's nothing to the Christian religion."

Recently I heard a Christian businessman say, "I don't want to open my store on Sunday, but my competitors open their stores and I must meet this competition." I think if I were this man I would take a big ad in the newspaper and say, "Regardless of what other stores do, we will not open on Sunday. We don't think it's right to desecrate the Lord's Day and keep our employees out of church. We will not open, even though we fail. We will give you good merchandise and the very best service the other six days of the week." Do you think such a course would meet failure? No, I believe God and good Christians would see that it didn't. Hold your standards high and God will see you through.

Today the world says, "Everybody is doing it. You must do it, too, or be left behind." So we see many Christians indulging in the things that all sinners do. But the true and faithful Christian will say, "Christ taught me to live up to the highest standard and I'm going to do that."

One of my Christian friends attended a business conference where alcoholic beverages were served. He told me that he and one other man, a faithful deacon, were the only ones there who turned down the liquor and drank "cokes." They were holding up the standard.

Often we lower our Christian standards in the realm of the spirit. We carry hatred in our hearts, we have the wrong attitude toward others, we commit sins of the disposition. If you don't have a love in your heart for everybody, there is something wrong with your Christianity. Dr. F. B. Meyer was a prominent preacher in London. Great throngs came to hear him preach every Sunday. Later Dr. G. Campbell Morgan came to town and served a church there. Soon the people were drawn to him and away from Meyer. Dr. Meyer's Christianity was put to the supreme test. He had the right spirit, however, for he said, "The only way I could conquer my feelings would be for me to pray for Dr. Morgan." And this he did and the waning Meyer became a greater and more prominent Meyer. But Satan does his best to get us to lower our standards.

6. *He wants you to criticize the church.* The only agency in the world that is today fighting Satan and his work is a true gospel-preaching church. When Satan sees a dead church, one that is just going through the forms of religion, he sits on the steeple and laughs. But when he sees a church on fire for God, winning souls and blessing lives, he gets busy.

Look at the methods that he uses. First, he attacks from the outside and only causes the church to grow stronger than ever. He tried that method after Pentecost and the church became more powerful and more united after each

The Devil Will Get You If You Don't Watch Out 39

of his attacks. What does he do next? He goes on the inside of the church and enters certain members. They start finding fault, they begin a whispering campaign, they put doubts in the minds of the members. Thus the work of the church is hurt.

God bless the Christian who loves his church and stands up for it. It isn't what it ought to be, but it is the best thing God has on this earth. It is nearer to the heart of Christ than anything else. Don't let the devil get in you and cause you to hurt the Lord's church. It won't go well with you if you criticize the church.

7. *He wants you to lose your temper.* Christ took all that they said and did to Him, yet He opened not His mouth. But let the least thing happen to us and we "blow our tops." We don't look much like the lowly Jesus when we do that, do we? The Bible says, "He that is slow to anger is better than the mighty; and he that ruleth his spirit than he that taketh a city" (Proverbs 16:32).

8. *He wants you to act childishly.* The Bible tells us to be "childlike," but we are never to act childishly. Yet, so many Christians are guilty along these lines.

Any man who has served as pastor of a church for any length of time can point out scores of people who quit the church and left the Lord's service because of their little, petty, childish disposition.

"I don't like what the preacher said last Sunday," they say. "I don't like the way the deacons run things," they say. "They failed to put me on a Sunday school committee," they say. And so they turn their backs upon Christ and the church and go out into the world to live absolutely Godless lives.

Don't let Satan fool you. Stand up and say, "I belong to Jesus. It matters not what others do or say, I am not going to act in a childish manner. I am going to remain faithful, whatever happens."

9. *He wants you to put off the matter of serving Christ.* Our churches have so many people who say, "Someday I am

going to quit being just a nominal church member. I am really going to serve the One who died for me." Yet you postpone the matter, the years roll by, and your opportunities pass away. This makes the devil very happy.

The great Scottish preacher, Alexander Maclaren visited one day in a certain home. The mother in that home said, "I am so miserable and unhappy. I have done so little for Jesus. When I was a girl I promised to serve Him, but I have given Him so little service." "What have you done?" asked the preacher. She replied, "I have cooked three meals a day, washed the dishes and cared for the children. But I did so want to do something for Jesus." "How many children do you have?" the preacher asked. "I have four boys, they are named after the gospels, Matthew, Mark, Luke and John."

Then the preacher asked, "Where is Matthew?" "You know he is a missionary in China."

"Where is Mark?" he asked. "He is a missionary in Africa. Your church sent him out." "Where is Luke?" he asked. "You know he is with his brother in China," she replied. "And what about John?" the preacher asked. She said, "Just this morning he told me he felt God had called him to preach also." The preacher smiled and said, "And so you've wasted your life. I would like to have your mansion in heaven and be as close to the throne as you will be."

Now God may not call you to serve in the limelight, He may want you to serve in an obscure place. But if you let the devil keep you from serving Christ, you will miss the greatest joy of your life.

IV. How Can We Defeat the Devil?

1. *We defeat him by staying close to Christ.* One time Satan had a battle with Christ and the Lord knocked him out. He respects Jesus' power. So if you stay close to Christ, you'll be safe from the devil.

2. *We defeat him by resisting him.* The Bible says, "Resist the devil, and he will flee from you" (James 4:7). Too many of us tolerate him, then we move closer to him, then

we embrace him. If when he first whispers to us, we resist him in the power of the Spirit, we can overcome him. But give him an inch and an entry and he will soon overcome you.

A woman bought a new dress which her husband could not afford. When he rebuked her she said, "But I was sorely tempted." The husband said, "Why didn't you say, 'Get thee behind me, Satan?'" She replied, "I did say that, and the devil got behind me and said, 'It fits so well in the back, you ought to get it.'"

Now, that isn't the way to resist Satan. We must say, "Satan, I belong to Jesus. I am going down His road. Get out of the way."

3. *We defeat him by getting busy for God.* "An idle brain is the devil's workshop." If you fill your time and life with God's service, you won't have any time left to serve the devil.

4. *We defeat him by trusting God's strength for our deliverance.* We are not to try to win the battle alone. The devil is mightier than we are. We'll lose out every time if we fight him alone. We must call for God's help when we are tempted.

A little boy asked his father, "Is the devil bigger and stronger than I am?" "Yes," answered the father. "Is he bigger and stronger than you are?" asked the boy. "Yes," answered the father, "much bigger and much stronger." "Well," asked the boy, "is he bigger and stronger than Jesus?" "No," replied the father. "All right," said the boy, "then I won't care a rap for him." And you and I need not be afraid of him if we lean upon the Lord's mighty arm.

Well, the devil is busy now, and he often overcomes us. But one day his evil career will be over. Christ will come back, cast Satan into the lake of fire and we shall be free forever.

Years ago a terrific storm swept our Northwest Coast. Rumors soon spread that the lighthouse had gone down in the storm. But a few days later the lighthouse keeper was seen on the streets of the city. Someone said to him, "We heard that the lighthouse went down in the storm." "Oh, no," said the man. "It was the worst storm we ever had, but in the midst of it all the lighthouse never shook."

That's it, my friends. Rest your case in the hands of the Lord Jesus, and the devil can never get you. That is a foundation that has never been shaken. He is a Friend who has never been defeated.

4

GOD'S FAVORITE WORD

Isaiah 1:18

Suppose that in tomorrow's mail you received an engraved invitation from the White House, which read as follows: "The President of the United States invites you to be his guest for dinner at the White House on the night of April 10th. Other guests will be the Queen of England, the Chief Justice of the Supreme Court and other noted figures. The President sincerely hopes that you can be present. R.S.V.P."

You would be proud indeed to receive such an invitation. You would show it to all of your friends. You would keep it to show to your children and grandchildren.

Well, One greater than the president has issued you an invitation. The King of heaven invites you to be His guest. He promises you the finest things on this earth and in the life beyond. He is the Greatest Inviter. All through the Bible He is standing with outstretched arms, crying unto men, "Come unto Me." This is His favorite word, the word "Come." It's a simple word, but all the wonders of heaven and earth are wrapped up in it.

Yes, God invites you to come to Him through faith in His Son, who said, "No man cometh unto the Father, but by me." Oh, won't you say in the words of the song:

"I will arise and go to Jesus,
He will embrace me in His arms;
In the arms of my dear Saviour,
Oh, there are ten thousand charms"?
— *Robert Robinson*

Let us look at some of the times when the word "come" is used in the Bible.

I. "Come Down"

One day Jesus was passing through Jericho (Luke 19:1-11). A little man named Zaccheus lived there. He was a stingy, grasping, miserly publican. He worked for his country's enemy, collecting exorbitant taxes for them and keeping plenty for himself. He had riches but he was not happy. The people hated him. He was a lonely man with no peace in his heart. But he had heard that this strange man, Jesus, loved all kinds of people. So when Jesus came to Jericho, Zaccheus rushed out to see Him. But Zaccheus was a man of little stature and he couldn't see Jesus for the crowd. So he climbed up in a sycamore tree to get a glimpse of the Saviour. Soon Jesus stopped under that very tree and looked up at Zaccheus. "Come down, Zaccheus," Jesus said. "I am going home with you today." So Zaccheus hurried down and took Jesus home for dinner. So moved was he by the presence of Christ that he said, "Lord, I'll give half of all I have to the poor. And if I have cheated any man I will pay him back fourfold." What a change Jesus made in this man's life!

People today want to see the Saviour, but they climb the wrong tree. They trust in their church membership, their gifts, their good works, their character. But Jesus says to them all, "If you want salvation, come down. Come down to Me." The lost man must come down in humility, acknowledging his sin, his need of a Saviour, his hopeless and helpless condition before God.

During a revival in a certain place a man went forward and knelt at the altar. A little boy whispered to his mother, "He won't be saved yet." "Why?" asked the mother. The boy replied, "He is kneeling on just one knee." He meant that the man had not fully humbled himself in repentance toward God. To be saved, one must come down.

In 1829 George Wilson of Pennsylvania was sentenced to be hanged for murder. But President Jackson issued him a pardon. Wilson refused to accept the pardon, saying that he was guilty and wanted to die. The case was carried all the way to the Supreme Court, which decreed that a pardon was of no value unless it was accepted. So George Wilson went to his death.

The Lord Jesus has issued us a pardon. It is signed and sealed in His own precious blood. But that pardon has no value for us unless we feel that we need it and unless we come to Him in humility, gratefully accepting that pardon. To be saved, to become a Christian, a man must "come down."

II. "COME FORTH"

This invitation is pictured in the story of Lazarus. He had been in his grave four days before Jesus came to the cemetery. The Saviour cried out, "Lazarus, come forth." Death could not hold him when the Son of God spoke, so Lazarus came out alive. Now before we are saved we are just as dead in sin as Lazarus was dead physically. Ephesians 2:1 tells us that sinners are "dead in trespasses and sins." It is only as Jesus calls us to come forth from our dead and sinful condition that we are regenerated.

He came to give His life for dead men. When we accept Him as Saviour and Lord, we pass from the realm of darkness and death to the realm of light and life. We call this "regeneration." The Bible calls it being "born again." In order to fit us for the kingdom of heaven, God must change us. If we kept the old original Adamic nature, we would be out of place in heaven. So God gives us a new nature. The process of regeneration causes us to become sons of God, changes our nature and fits us for heaven.

Regulus was a Roman citizen who was captured by the Carthaginians. Knowing his power with the Roman senate, Carthage sent him back to Rome to secure certain legislation. He made a vow to return to Carthage, whatever it might cost him. When he went to Rome he advised the senate against this legislation, saying he would rather die than see Rome humiliated. True to his pledge he returned to Carthage. The Carthaginians cut off his eyelids and tied him on his back with the blazing sun shining into his eyes. He died a horrible death. He had the glory of the sun, but since his eyes were not adapted to it, he was blinded.

So if unregenerate men went up to heaven and beheld the glory of God, it would be torment to them. Regeneration brings adaptation, and fits a man to behold God's glory. It introduces us into the divine life and introduces the divine life into us.

III. "Come Unto . . ."

Here we see Jesus looking upon the multitudes and saying, "Come unto me, all ye that labour and are heavy laden, and I will give you rest" (Matthew 11:28). Jesus not only saves, but He fully satisfies. Some Christians do not believe this, so they drink from the stagnant pools of this world, when they could be quenching their thirst in the sparkling waters of the Fountain of Life.

Dr. Vance Havner says that "the heels follow where the heart goes." This is why some people go to the house of the Lord for satisfaction. Their hearts belong to Jesus and their heels take them to worship Him and hear more about Him. There are too many Sunday morning Christians who feel it their duty to attend church once a week, but they are not satisfied there because they give the rest of the week to the attractions of the world. They are too good to leave the church out entirely, but they are too bad to leave the world of sin out entirely.

A man's Christianity can be judged by the things that satisfy him. If a man gets three square meals at home, he doesn't need to go to a restaurant and order steak and pork chops or the blue plate special. And when a man's nature is satisfied with the things of Christ, he doesn't run around eating husks from Satan's trough.

Yes, Jesus fully satisfies. If you are not satisfied, come to Him in full surrender and He will fill your life with true satisfaction.

IV. "Come Out . . ."

In II Corinthians 6:17 we read, "Wherefore come out from among them, and be ye separate, saith the Lord, and touch not the unclean thing; and I will receive you."

The child of God is never happy, nor can he expect the

God's Favorite Word

best blessings or greatest power, as long as he holds on to the things which God opposes. But God promises everything to the one who leaves his sin and gives his best to Jesus.

Listen to Matthew 6:33: "But seek ye first the kingdom of God, and his righteousness; and all these things shall be added unto you."

Listen to Psalm 84:11: "For the Lord God is a sun and shield: the Lord will give grace and glory: no good thing will he withhold from them that walk uprightly."

Listen to Romans 8:32: "He that spared not his own Son, but delivered him up for us all, how shall he not with him also freely give us all things?"

Now we are to be careful about this matter of separation. If we separate ourselves from unbelievers and the works of the devil, we must do it in a spirit of humility and love. If we regard ourselves as better than others, we become nothing but holier-than-thou Pharisees and Jesus despised them. We are never to say, "I'm better than you, you need to clean up your life." The one you are criticizing and advising may be a thousand times better than you.

Sins of the disposition are as bad as sins of the flesh. Your criticism, your self-righteousness, your Pharisaism is a sin of the disposition and is often worse than a sin of the flesh. Some people would not dare to smoke, take a drink or go to a picture show, but they will not hesitate to hate someone, to talk about them, to hurt them, to lie about them.

I am thinking now of a woman who talks often of her own goodness. She is better than anyone else because she doesn't do this thing or that thing which someone else does. She is continually talking about someone else. If you took an X-ray of her jaw you would get a moving picture. Her life is not sweet and useful.

Yes, the Christian must separate himself from the world, but it must be a separation unto God, unto good works, unto a sweet disposition and a humble attitude. Some modernists whom we know surpass us in sweetness of spirit. We know the truth as it is in Jesus. We believe all that the Bible says about Him. Let us bear this truth about in the precious vessel of a sweet spirit, not in looking down on and criticizing others.

It is said that the Tigris River flows straight through a certain lake, yet the river does not mingle its waters with the water of the lake. It retains a taste and color different from the lake. We Christians must be like that. We are not to take on the color of the world, we are to retain the likeness of Christ. Some fish live in a salty sea, but their flesh is not salty. Pearls live in dark ocean caves, but they are not black. So we can live in a sinful world, yet not be of that world. We must endure its evils, but we are not to be injured by them.

V. "Come After . . ."

Jesus said, "If any man will come after me, let him deny himself, and take up his cross, and follow me" (Matthew 16:24). We sing, "Where He leads me I will follow." Do we mean it? He will lead us into a fine life of service if we follow Him. He is ready to lead us. Are we willing to follow?

This leading comes from a study of God's Word and through the guidance of the Holy Spirit. The Bible tells us to be obedient, to serve the Lord, to bear fruit for Him. Are you following this leadership? Are you faithful to His Church? Are you a tither? Are you witnessing for Him? Has anyone been blessed, has anyone been saved because of you and your Christian life?

Are you following the Lord in the matter of your giving? The Bible teaches us to give "tithes and offerings." The faithful tither pays his tithe through his church. Out of his offerings, over and above the tithe, he can give to other worthwhile causes. No Christian ever goes far down the road of faithful stewardship until he puts selfishness and material things under foot and gives God what is rightfully His.

Who were the disciples of the New Testament? They were men who met Jesus and followed Him. You have met Jesus — are you following Him?

When a great missionary walked down the street, someone said, "There is Jesus Christ's man." Can anyone say that of you?

VI. "COME WITH . . ."

In the Song of Solomon the bridegroom says to the bride, "Come with me." Jesus says to His bride, the church, the saints of God, "Come with Me and let us enjoy the sweetest fellowship."

A great pianist said, "If I miss one day of practice, I notice it in my playing. If I miss two days my friends notice it. If I miss three days the public notices it." So if we neglect fellowship with Jesus it affects our service. We may go ahead, we may be busy with the mechanics of religion, but we soon get far away from the Lord and our service proves barren and unfruitful.

A poor man had a dear little girl whom he loved very much, but he was unable to give her all that he would like to give her. A rich couple offered to care for her and give her everything if she would come and live with them. The father told her all about the offer and said, "Don't you think you had better go and live with them?" The little girl exclaimed, "Why, father, don't you want me?" "Yes," he answered, "but they can give you so many things that I can't." The little girl threw her arms around her father's neck and said, "But, daddy, I wouldn't have you." And although we may gain the world, nothing takes the place of Jesus. Every day we ought to get alone with Him and just love Him and enjoy His fellowship.

VII. "COME UP"

When John, the beloved disciple, was on the Isle of Patmos, he said that a door in heaven opened up and he heard a voice like unto a trumpet, saying, "Come up." This reminds us of that which will happen when Jesus comes in the air. The Lord Himself shall descend from heaven and call us up to be with Him forever. This experience is known as the "rapture." At that time Jesus will take His people, the church, out of this world and into His own wonderful presence. What a day that will be! The dictionary defines "rapture" as "extreme pleasure or delight, ecstasy, enthusiasm." Nothing can ever compare to the rapture that will be ours when we shall be delivered from this world and its care and when we are taken up to be with Jesus and our loved ones, world without end.

Some of us are growing old. Our eyesight is not as keen as it once was, we don't hear as well, our step is not as light. Some of us have hair that has turned gray, some have hair that has turned out. But what does that matter? We'll all be young when He comes, we'll all be like Him.

They say that I am growing old.
I've heard them tell it times untold
But I'm not growing old!
This frail, old shell in which I dwell
Is growing old, I know full well,
But I am not the shell.

What if my hair is turning grey?
Grey hairs are honorable, they say.
What if my eyesight's growing dim?
I still can see to follow Him,
Who sacrificed His life for me
Upon the Cross of Calvary!

What should I care if Time's old plow
Has left its furrows on my brow?
Another house, not made with hand
Awaits me in the Glory Land.
What tho' I falter in my walk?
What tho' my tongue refuse to talk?
I still can tread the Narrow Way —
I still can watch and praise and pray!

My hearing may not be as keen
As in the past it may have been.
Still, I can hear my Saviour say
In whispers soft, "This is the way."
The inward man, the Scriptures say,
Is growing stronger every day.
Then how can I be growing old
When safe within my Saviour's fold?

Ere long my soul shall fly away
And leave this tenement of clay.
This robe of flesh I'll drop, and rise

God's Favorite Word

To seize the everlasting prize —
I'll meet you on the Streets of Gold
And prove that I'm not growing old!

Oh, what a prospect for the Christian! What a blessed hope! Wars may rage, storms may come, sorrows may sweep over the soul. But the Christian can look up and say, "I have Christ, I have a hope, I have a home in heaven because of Him."

On the coast of England there is a dangerous place called Eddystone Rock. It is often swept with violent storms. Many ships have been dashed to pieces against the Rock. Even the most strongly constructed lighthouses have been destroyed soon after they were built. Years ago a great architect named Winstaney was challenged to build a lighthouse that would stand up against the fury of the storms. He was very proud of his work, so he put this inscription on the lighthouse:

> Blow, ye winds,
> Rise, ye ocean,
> Break forth, ye elements,
> And try my work.

One night when a great storm threatened, Winstanley was so confident that he volunteered to spend the night in the lighthouse. That night the storm broke in all of its fury and both the lighthouse and the architect were destroyed. He trusted the work of his own hands and was destroyed with it.

Then another architect named Smeaton, a great Christian, was commissioned to design another lighthouse. He built it of stone. It seemed to be a very part of the Rock itself. The inscription he placed on it came from the Bible, "Except the Lord build the house, they labour in vain that build it." The storms came, the winds blew, the rains fell, but the lighthouse stood. It had a firm foundation.

How are you building your life? Build upon the things of this world and you will fail and fall. But come, come, come, build upon Christ and your life will stand the test of time and eternity.

My hope is built on nothing less,
Than Jesus' blood and righteousness;
I dare not trust the sweetest frame,
But wholly lean on Jesus' Name.
  On Christ, the solid Rock, I stand;
All other ground is sinking sand.
— *Edward Mote*

5

THE MOST PROFITABLE BUSINESS IN THE WORLD

I Timothy 4:8

Some of God's most faithful servants have suffered greatly. We think of John the Baptist, who came preaching in the wilderness, and baptizing in the River Jordan. He attracted great crowds of people who later left him and followed Jesus. But he said, "He must increase, but I must decrease" (John 3:30). He was not only a great and faithful preacher, but he had the right spirit. But what happened? He was beheaded by Herod. Did it pay him to serve Jesus?

We think of Stephen, the wonderful and faithful deacon. He went out to preach Christ and they stoned him to death. Did it pay him to serve Christ? We think of Paul. He gave up everything to follow Christ. Just after his conversion, Ananias, led by the Spirit, was sent to tell him "how great things he must suffer" for Christ's name's sake (Acts 9:16). And Paul did suffer. He was beaten often, he was shipwrecked, he knew hunger and thirst and cold. He spent much time in jail and (according to tradition) was finally beheaded. Did it pay him to serve Jesus?

We think of the beloved Apostle John, who loved Jesus and leaned on His bosom at the Last Supper. He preached Christ for fifty or sixty years, then was banished to Patmos in his old age. There he is alone on that lonely island, longing to see Jesus. Did it pay him to serve Jesus?

The answer to all of these questions is an unequivocal "Yes." For, although these men suffered greatly, God brought them out and crowned them with honor and glory and gave them a big place in heaven. He gave them a big place in history, also. We don't remember those who persecuted them, but after nearly two thousand years John the Baptist and Stephen and Paul and John have their names written high on the roll of the world's greatest men.

So I want to tell you that the most profitable business in the world is the business of serving God. It pays here and hereafter. Now let me ask you some questions.

I. Does It Pay for a Christian to Pray?

I know that sometimes we pray for something and nothing happens. Then we are prone to say, "Oh, what's the use?" We are saying that prayer doesn't pay, but it does. Often it helps us to get what we need, often it makes us see that we don't need what we ask for. God knows always what is best for us. Sometimes He answers "yes," because that is best for us. Sometimes He answers "no," because that is best for us. Sometimes He tells us to wait a while and that is best for us. But in every case God answers true prayer.

Look at the first church yonder in Jerusalem. There came a day when some of their preachers were arrested and threatened with harm if they kept on preaching Christ. When they were released they called the church together and told the members what had happened. And what did they do? They didn't make a protest to the authorities. They were no match for the government. All the powers of society were against them. There was only one thing left for them to do and they did it. They prayed.

And what happened? Acts 4:31-33:

> And when they had prayed, the place was shaken where they were assembled together; and they were all filled with the Holy Ghost, and they spake the word of God with boldness. And the multitude of them that believed were of one heart and of one soul: neither said any of them that ought of the things which he possessed was his own; but they had all things common. And with great power gave the apostles witness of the resurrection of the Lord Jesus: and great grace was upon them all.

The Most Profitable Business in the World 55

It paid them to pray and it pays us. When God called me to preach, my prospects were not very bright. I had only two years of a high school education, I had a family to support. My only speaking experience had been in the young people's group in our church. But I prayed. That was about all I could do. And God gave me a start and brought me through. He made it possible for me to finish my high school, college and seminary education. Oh, He answered my prayers a thousand times. I know it pays.

Now no kind of prayer is as effective as private, personal prayer. You may lead a public prayer in church and you are praying in behalf of others who are there. But it's when you get alone with God that you can really pour out your heart. After a great meeting in Boston the newspaper report wrote this: "The prayer of Dr. So-and-So was one of the most eloquent ever offered to a New England audience." Maybe our audience does affect our public prayers, but when you are alone with God, there is no one to hear you but Him and you can really pray. Yes, it does pay to pray.

II. Does It Pay to Obey God?

In Deuteronomy 28 God tells Moses how He will bless the people if they are obedient to Him. He says that those who live in the city and those who are farmers in the field will prosper if they will only keep His commandments. Then He says a striking thing. "And the Lord shall make thee the head, and not the tail; and thou shalt be above only, and not beneath" (Deuteronomy 28:13). The same thing applies today. If we obey God we will be winners, if we disobey Him we will be losers.

When Moses was leading Israel toward the Promised Land, he had trouble with the Amalekites. These people carried on guerilla warfare against Israel. They sniped at them from the rear and killed those who fell behind. And God said, "I will punish the Amalekites." Well, the time came when Saul was king and God said to him, "I remember the sin of the Amalekites. Now I want you to destroy them and all their property and all their cattle." So Saul went into battle with them and won the victory. Later Samuel came along. The preacher often comes at the most inopportune time. He didn't say a word but Saul spoke up and said, "I did all that God commanded, I slew the Amalekites." Right then some sheep began to bleat and the oxen began lowing and gave the king away. The preacher asked, "If you destroyed as God told you to destroy, what is that noise I hear." "Oh," said the king, "we brought some of the cattle home to be sacrificed to the Lord." But Samuel said, "That's not the thing. God told you to destroy the cattle and to obey is better than sacrifice." (See I Samuel 15.)

Samuel was simply saying that nothing in the world can take the place of obedience to God. If God is telling you to do a certain thing, nothing else can take the place of that thing. For instance, God calls a man to preach and he says, "No, I won't preach. I'll go into business instead and make money and give that others might preach." But that is not obedience. If God wants you to speak to an unsaved person and you say, "I'll not do that, but I'll make an extra gift so someone else can be employed to do it," that is not obedience.

Some people claim to have been born again, but they won't obey Christ in baptism and they won't obey Him in church membership. They will never mean much to the cause of Christ. But it pays to obey God in all things.

III. Does It Pay to Tithe?

God answers that in Malachi 3:10: "Bring ye all the tithes into the storehouse, that there may be meat in mine house, and prove me now herewith, saith the Lord of hosts, if I will not open you the windows of heaven, and pour you out a blessing, that there shall not be room enough to receive it."

My personal experience tells me that it pays to tithe. When I finished college and seminary I was called to a small church at a small salary. I owed a large sum of money, I had a family to support. I asked myself the question, "Is it right to put my tithe in the church when I owe so much money?" Then the thought came to me, "I owe God more than I owe anyone else. He is my preferred creditor. Besides this, He

The Most Profitable Business in the World

has said that He would take care of us and provide every need if we put Him first." So every Sunday my tithe went into the offering plate and the blessings began to flow. I was able to pay my debts much sooner than I expected. God kept His promise.

I am thinking of a man who moved to the city and joined the church of which I was pastor. He heard me preach on tithing, but declared that he couldn't see it. He bought a fine home and a nice car. Suddenly, for no apparent reason, he lost his job. He finally found a job in another state and he said to me before he left, "I have certainly learned one thing here. From now on I'm going to tithe."

A letter from one of my former members told me of sickness and debts and doctor bills. He said, "I believe all of this has come upon us because we failed to tithe when God prospered us." I could not answer dogmatically, but I began to think about the matter. I arrived at the conclusion that I had never known a tither who did not pay his debts. Sickness and extra expense came to some of them, but they were always able to take care of their debts.

I am thinking of two men in the armed service. They have the same rank, they receive the same pay. But one doesn't tithe. He is always in trouble, always in debt. The other is a faithful tither. He and his family have all they need and their home is free of debt. I believe firmly that tithing has made the difference. Yes, it pays to tithe. God said so and I believe it.

IV. Does It Pay to Say "No"?

This is about the hardest little word in the English language for many of us to use. Daniel was taken to Babylon and placed in a school with other young men to be trained for the king's service. Daniel and his three friends who were faithful to God were given wine to drink and pork to eat. But Daniel said, "We cannot eat and drink these things. It is against our religious convictions." Their teacher said, "If you refuse this meat and drink, you won't look as good as the other children and the king will cut my head off." Daniel replied, "Just test us for several days and see how things come out." So for ten days they didn't eat the king's food, but held to their convictions. At the end of that time they were better looking in every way than the other children and when they were examined as to wisdom and understanding they were found to be ten times wiser than the magicians and astrologers of the country. It paid them to say, "No."

Young people, you need to learn to say "No." Some of you girls go out with boys, and you unwisely allow them to indulge in certain intimacies. Before long they are asking you to prove your love for them by going even farther. You think you will lose him if you don't give in. But, oh, the sorrow and tragic consequences that result when you do give in! You must learn to say "No" to anything that borders on indecency.

You young men must also learn to say "No." You have your first job and you want to get ahead, you want to stand in with the boss. When you attend your first office party, you are going to be urged to drink. Can you say "No" or do you think you have to be "one of the boys"? Many a drunkard's career began with just that one drink.

Some years ago, when radio was in its infancy, a young Southern man developed into one of the greatest sports announcers in the country. He went all over America broadcasting the principal sporting events. His rich Southern brogue and his colorful language made every sports event a pleasure to listen to. Then he dropped out of the broadcasting picture and I wondered where he was. One day I was in my brother's office and he called me over to the window. He pointed out a dissipated man ambling down the street under the influence of liquor. I asked him who it was and he gave me the name of the former famous radio announcer. He had not learned to say "No" and that brought about his pitiful downfall.

The strong man is the man who says "No." The weakling goes along with the crowd.

The Most Profitable Business in the World

V. Does It Pay to Turn From Backsliding?

What is a backslider? It is a person who has been saved, who knows the Lord, who was once faithful to Him, but who now lives as if he never knew Him. A backslider is cold and indifferent to the Church, and Christ is thrust into the background. And many of our church members fall into this category. This situation becomes one of the saddest aspects of a pastor's life. He rejoices to see one active for the Lord, then his heart breaks as later on he sees that one living a backslidden life.

Who is the unhappiest man in the world? It is a man who once knew the joy of salvation, who once walked with the Lord, who once tasted the sweetness of Christian fellowship, who once enjoyed his church and his service for the Lord. But now he is back out in the world, having turned his back upon God. I say that he is the unhappiest man in the world.

But here is good news for the backslider. In Jeremiah 3:12 we read, "Go and proclaim these words toward the north, and say, Return, thou backsliding Israel, saith the Lord; and I will not cause mine anger to fall upon you: for I am merciful, saith the Lord, and I will not keep my anger for ever." You may have moved away from God, you may have turned your back upon Him and His church. But He is still waiting with open arms to take you back.

David backslid into deepest sin, but God forgave him and restored His joy to him when he repented. Peter backslid but God forgave him and made him over when he repented. And He will receive you if you will only confess your sin and ask him to forgive you.

Jacob went out from home, a fugitive from Esau's anger. That first night he slept under the stars and he had a dream. In the dream he saw a ladder reaching from earth to heaven. Angels were going up and down the ladder and the Lord was standing above it. Jacob heard God make him a wonderful promise. When he waked he made a high and holy vow to follow the Lord. He called the place Bethel, "the house of God." But Jacob got out into the world and let the world get into him. He became rich through some shady deals, he raised a large family. Then, when his enemies were about to destroy him, God said to him, "Jacob, get back to Bethel."

Well, where could Jacob go? He couldn't go to Laban, his father-in-law, who was angry with him. He couldn't go to his brother, Esau, because he had cheated Esau. There was just one place to go, back to Bethel, back to God. Oh, Jacob, don't you remember Bethel? Don't you remember the ladder, the angels? Don't you remember God's promise and your holy vow? You're not happy now, Jacob, because you're not living for God. You must go back to Bethel and a new experience with the Lord. And Jacob did go back and God met him again there at Bethel. He was never the same again. He made up with his brother, God protected him from his enemies, but the best part of it all was that he had an intimate touch with God that lasted him the rest of his life.

Oh, backslider, where can you go? Where can you find peace and happiness? Go back to Bethel, go back to God, go back to church, go back to a life of faithful service to Him. It will pay as nothing else.

Dr. Harold Dye of California was preaching one day on the Cross to a group of Spanish-speaking people. He asked the question, "What would you have done if you had been in the crowd that day when Jesus fell beneath the cross?" Later a little eight-year-old Mexican boy came up to him and said, "Please, sir, I would have helped Him carry it." "But," said the preacher, "if you had done that the cruel Roman soldiers would have beaten you until the blood ran down your back." The boy looked up and said, "I don't care, I would have helped him carry the cross just the same."

Two weeks later Dr. Dye stood at the door of the church, speaking to the people as they went out. He patted little Pedro on the back and the boy shrank back with a little cry. "Don't do that, please, sir," he said, "my back is sore." The preacher took the boy back into the cloak room and took

The Most Profitable Business in the World

off his shirt. To his horror and amazement the boy's back was criss-crossed with bloody welts. "Who did this?" the preacher asked, and the boy replied, "My mother did it because I came to church."

Oh, when I think of others who suffer for Jesus because they love Him, I wonder why we are so cold and unfaithful and indifferent. Let me call you from your backslidden ways and coldness of heart to a new dedication of life to Christ. It will surely pay you to return from your backsliding.

Does it pay to serve Christ? Yes, but the best is yet to come. The biggest part of our pay lies out yonder in the future. Someday we'll drop this robe of flesh and soar out beyond the stars. Waiting at the gate will be the One who loved us and died for us and saved us. Oh, when we see Him, when we hear His voice, when we thank Him for bringing us safely home, that will be glory, glory, glory all the way!

Then truly we shall say, "It paid to trust Christ and follow Him. It paid on earth and it will pay in heaven as long as the ages roll." Yes, this is the most profitable business on earth. Are you engaged in it?

6

SOWING AND REAPING

Galatians 6:7

We live in a day of spiritual forgetfulness. Men are forgetting God and His Son. They are forgetting His Church. They are forgetting that the Lord's Day is really His Day. They are forgetting death and the terrible fact of judgment. But the awful fact remains that they must pay for their neglect and forgetfulness. They must reap what they sow. This is the unchangeable law of nature and of God. Men may forget God and all that this forgetfulness involves, but one day they must reap the fearful harvest.

"Whatsoever a man soweth, that shall he also reap." There is no truer text in the Bible. But even if these words were not in the Bible, we know they are true. We know from experience. We have sown and the reaping time has come. We know that "whatsoever a man soweth, that shall he also reap."

I. THE FIRST TRUTH IN THE TEXT: "GOD IS NOT MOCKED"

The apostle is simply saying, "You can't fool God. You can't sin and get away with it." You can't fool God because He sees all and knows all. You can hide from people, but you can't hide from God. Your family, your friends, your neighbors, may not even suspect your sin, but God knows all about it. He sees you in the brightness of the midday, He sees you in the blackness of the midnight. He sees all. You must account to Him for everything.

A man took his little boy into a neighbor's field to steal

potatoes. Before putting the potatoes in a bag the man looked in every direction, north, south, east, west. Then the little fellow very wisely said, "Daddy, you forgot to look one way, you forgot to look up." And we are like that. We are careful that others not see us sin. But God sees, God knows.

Then you can't fool God because He has all power. He can make you or break you. You are clay in His hand. He can give you life or take it away. The whole earth is in His hands. He speaks and it is done. The winds and the waves obey His will. As God has all power over nature, He has all power over you.

He has power to bring you to judgment. In Revelation 6:16 we are told that in the awful day of judgment men will pray for the rocks and the mountains to fall upon them and hide them from the wrath of the Lamb. This will not happen but even if it did, God in His mighty power would overturn every rock and every mountain and bring men out to judgment.

That's the kind of a God He is. You must live under His all-seeing eye and you must face Him someday. Oh, how foolish is the man who thinks he can live as he pleases and escape the judgments of an Almighty God.

Many years ago I was preaching in my first revival. A delivery boy who was bringing some groceries into the kitchen of one of our members was invited by her to attend the revival services. He looked out of the window and said, "Oh, I can't come, it's going to rain." And she replied, "It won't be raining on the judgment day."

What a sobering thought! You can make all kinds of excuses now, but these excuses will not help you on the judgment day. You are sowing now, you will reap then.

II. THE SECOND TRUTH IN THE TEXT: YOU REAP WHAT YOU SOW

1. *We reap in our daily lives what we sow right here.* Mr. Moody once preached on "Sowing and Reaping" and gave several illustrations to prove the point. At the conclu-

sion of his sermon a man stood up and shouted, "I don't believe it." Right then two detectives who were searching for the man closed in on him and arrested him for a crime he had committed. Surely he came to believe that "whatsoever a man soweth, that shall he also reap."

Some years ago, in a small Southern town, I preached a sermon on this text. After the service I talked to a young man in the church about his salvation and he sneered at the idea of Christ and salvation. The next morning, when I came down to breakfast, I was told that some officers had come to town early that morning and had arrested that young man for stealing a car. He, too, I am sure, learned that "whatsoever a man soweth, that shall he also reap."

2. *We reap in the lives of others what we sow here.* Herein is the tragedy of sin. It not only hurts us, but it hurts others whom we love. The Bible tells us that the sins of the parents are visited upon the children, even down to the third generation. Many men sin and forget all about it, only to meet that sin's consequences later in the life of a loved one.

A man once gave a letter to a prominent evangelist, asking the preacher to read the letter carefully and pray for him. The letter read, "As a young man I lived an immoral life. Later on I married a wonderful girl and God gave us a precious baby. One day the baby became ill and we called in two doctors to examine her. We were greatly concerned. My wife and I waited downstairs for the report of the doctors. Soon one of them came down and asked me what kind of a life I had lived before marriage. I had to confess that I had lived a loose, immoral life. Then the doctor said, 'Come upstairs and see the consequences of that life.' He led me upstairs and, pointing to the baby, said, 'If your baby lives, she will go through life with a twisted spine and may lose her mind.' My God, preacher, I didn't know I would have to pay the price of my sin in the life of our baby."

Yes, sin hurts us, it hurts God, it often hurts those we love best in all the world.

Every mother and father owe at least two things in the spiritual realm to their children. First, you owe it to them

Sowing and Reaping

to live at your best for Christ. When the baby is born, just remember that it had nothing to do with its birth. You brought it into the world. So as the babe is laid in your arms, you ought to look up to God and say, "Oh, Lord, help me to live rightly before my little one."

Some parents are much more interested in worldly things than in spiritual matters. They are giving their time and energy to these material things instead of their children. You may neglect their spiritual welfare now, but someday you'll reap the results of this neglect. All those worldly organizations to which you are giving your life now may seem very important, but they are not nearly so important as the welfare of your children. That should come first.

The great evangelist, J. Wilbur Chapman, was holding a meeting in a certain place when a woman came to him and said, "My son is in prison in the next city to which you are going. Here is his name. Please visit him and try to win him to Christ." Dr. Chapman promised to do this, so when he arrived in the city he visited the boy and told him how anxious his mother was for him to accept Christ. The boy looked straight in the preacher's eyes and said, "Damn my mother." Dr. Chapman said, "Son, surely you don't mean that." The boy replied, "Yes, I do. When I was a boy she played cards instead of going to church. She taught me how to play. As I grew older I began to gamble. I lost large sums of money and finally I embezzled my employer's money to pay my gambling debts. That's why I am in prison. My mother is responsible for it all, so you can tell her just what I said."

Oh, mother and dad, what a responsibility is yours! How very important it is for you to live for Christ and set the right example for your children.

Then you owe it to your children to lead them to Christ. Don't let any preacher or Sunday school teacher rob you of that joy. Go to church and Sunday school with your children. Get them under the power of the Gospel. Then at the proper time take them aside and tell them of Jesus and their need of Him. We do everything else for them. We see that they eat the proper food and wear the right clothes and go to the best school. Why do we neglect the most important part of all?

In my first pastorate one of our members lived next door to the church. I begged her to help us to get her boy to the church and to Christ. She said, "I don't believe in trying to influence my boy in this way." But the world believed in influencing him and as he grew older he went out into sin and broke his mother's heart.

A certain father felt the same way about his boy. He said, "I don't believe in trying to influence him." The time came when the boy broke his arm and a Christian doctor was called upon to set it. Every other word the boy uttered was a curse word. The Christian doctor later went to the boy's father and said, "You didn't believe in influencing your boy, but the devil did. Now you must reap what you have sown."

If you have a garden and don't cultivate it and plant the right kind of seed, what will you get out of that garden? A crop of weeds, that's all. And if you don't plant the right seeds in the hearts and lives of your children, you'll raise up some human weeds that will choke off your happiness.

If your boy were lost in the darkness, what would you do? You would take a bright light and hold it high and lead him out of the darkness. Well, without Christ he is lost in the darkness of sin. You ought to hold high the light of a good Christian life and thus lead him from the darkness to the Saviour.

I visited an unsaved teen-age boy and he said to me, "I would like to confess Christ and join the church, but my parents tell me I must be sure I know what I am doing." He knew right from wrong, he knew how to make good grades in school, had been attending our church and Sunday school and he knew how to be saved. I investigated further and learned that his parents were backslidden church members. They had lived in our city for years but had never moved their church membership to town. They were as cold as ice, as indifferent as anyone could be. They had turned their backs upon the Lord and the Church. Now how could I

Sowing and Reaping

win that boy in the face of such parental indifference? You can neglect your Christian duty now and the welfare of your children, but someday you'll sit in sorrow because of it.

Oh, parents, live for Christ before your children, then lead them to the Saviour. You are sowing now, someday you must reap.

III. THE THIRD TRUTH IN THE TEXT — YOU REAP MORE THAN YOU SOW

This is a law of nature. If you sow one grain of wheat or one grain of corn, you naturally expect to reap more than you have sown.

Now the same thing is true in the spiritual realm. If we sow to the flesh we can expect to reap double. God has so arranged it that the sinner pays here and hereafter. "Be sure your sin will find you out." That's the way sin pays off here. "The wages of sin is death." That's the way sin pays off hereafter.

On the edge of one of our cities there is a large orphanage run by a fraternal organization. Some years ago a woman who was living in sin brought her two little girls to the orphanage. She said, "I want to leave them with you. I don't want them ever to find out the kind of life I am living." The years went by and the girls grew up. One day the police were called to a cheap hotel, where they found the older girl dying in sin. Her mother's blood was strong in her and she followed in the pathway she had trod. The mother was called in. She fell down by the bedside and cried out, "Oh, God, I sowed the seed, now I am reaping the harvest."

Some months later this mother was called to the hospital. Her younger daughter had gone the same route of sin. She had fallen in love with a fine boy, but when he learned of her sin, he jilted her. She went to the store where he worked and shot herself in front of him. In the hospital the mother had to stand by helplessly and watch her die. As the girl breathed her last breath the poor mother cried out, "Oh, God, I have sowed the seed, now I am reaping the double harvest."

Yes, it's true. We reap more than we sow. If we sow to

the flesh we will reap a double harvest of sorrow.

If we sow to the Spirit, we can expect to reap double there also. On this earth we will reap a clear conscience, peace in our hearts, sweet fellowship with Christ. Then in the life beyond we will have heaven and all it means. It will be "all this and heaven, too," if you live for Christ. It pays to serve Jesus, here and hereafter.

Before Sam Jones, the great Methodist preacher, became an evangelist, he was pastor of a small church in North Georgia. In one of his printed sermons he tells the story of two people in that community. A certain man lived a life of open sin. God had no part in his life. He cursed the church, Christians and preachers. He died one morning at three o'clock. At midnight he had called his wife and said, "I have just had an awful dream. I saw devils all over the room, ready to take my soul down to hell. Don't let them do it." She tried to quiet him, but could not. At three o'clock he died, crying out, "They're taking me to hell, they're taking me to hell." A man ought not to die like that. He doesn't have to die like that.

The other person was a fine Christian woman who lay near to death's door. When Mr. Jones visited her, she said, "Pastor, I'm not afraid to die, I have made my peace with God through Jesus Christ. But I am afraid of that last hour when death will come upon me." The pastor talked to her and prayed with her and sought to comfort her.

The next day Mr. Jones visited her again and she said, "After you left me yesterday I drifted off into sleep and I had a most wonderful dream. I dreamed that I was on the bank of a beautiful river. I looked across the river and saw many happy people there with some of my loved ones among them. I realized that I was looking into heaven. Then a boatman rowed across and invited me to get in his boat. We crossed the river and landed amid the shouts of the redeemed. Then an angel came and said, 'I am going to take you and introduce you to the king of the palace!' He took me to the throne room and as I entered I saw Someone coming toward me. He wore a white robe and on His face

Sowing and Reaping

was the sweetest smile. He came up and took my hand in His and as He did so I felt the prints of the nails in His hands. Then I knew that the King of the palace was Christ Jesus my Saviour."

The next day this woman called her husband to her bedside and said, "I feel so strangely sweet. What is it?" And he replied, "You are dying." "Then," she said, "kiss me goodby and let me go." And in a few minutes she had gone out into the "land that is fairer than day."

Oh, friends, that hour is coming for you and for me. Let's be careful to sow the right kind of seed, and in that day we won't have to worry about the harvest.

7

THE WORLD'S WORST DISEASE

Romans 3:23

There have been many tragic diseases in the world, diseases that have taken the lives of millions of people. Heart disease is our number one killer, cancer is next. You may never have cancer or a heart attack, but all of us are afflicted with one disease. It is the malady which the Bible calls *sin*. This disease affects everybody. It affects them for time and eternity.

Look at the world today. Think of all the crime and hatred and bloodshed and sin that fill the world. We see it on an individual basis, on a local basis. We see it on the state level and the national level. We see it on an international scale. What's the matter with the world in this enlightened age? The answer comes back from God's Word: "All have sinned, and come short of the glory of God." Now let me try to answer some questions about this thing called "sin."

I. What Is Sin?

1. *It is the transgression of the law.* "Whosoever committeth sin transgresseth also the law: for sin is the transgression of the law" (I John 3:4). What law? God's law, the law He gave at Sinai, the law that is spelled out in the Bible. The Ten Commandments and the Sermon on the Mount are included. All along God is saying, "Do this and don't do that." We know what the law is, we know how we ought to live. Yet we have transgressed the law.

The World's Worst Disease 71

Now that transgression may be great or small. When a motorist runs a red light, the court says, "You have transgressed man's law." When a man murders another man, the court says, "You have transgressed the law of the land." And when a man sins, whether that sin be great or small, God says, "You have transgressed My law, you have broken My commandment."

2. *I John 5:17 tells us that all unrighteousness is sin.* Now unrighteousness comes in many forms. Let me list a few: bad habits, complaining, covetousness, criticism, discouragement, forgetting God, gossip, hypocrisy, jealousy, persecution, pride, selfishness, unfaithfulness, worldliness.

When Moses was leading the children of Israel toward the Promised Land they began to grumble and complain against him, and God counted it as sin. We do sin when we complain against the providences of God. A certain woman was always grumbling. Then one year she had the best potato crop in the country. Her pastor said to her, "Surely you can't complain this time," as he complimented her on her fine crop. "Yes," she said, "I have a good crop, but there are no bad potatoes in the lot, so what am I going to feed the pigs?"

God gives us some other examples of unrighteousness. He says that a proud heart is sin (Proverbs 21:4). He says that a lustful look is sin (Matthew 5:28). He says that idle words are sinful (Matthew 12:36). He says that covetousness is sin (Colossians 3:5). He says that hatred is sin (I John 3:15).

3. *A lack of faith is sin.* This is the greatest of all sins, when one doesn't believe in God as Father and Christ as Saviour. This is the sin that condemns. John 3:18: "He that believeth on him is not condemned: but he that believeth not is condemned already, because he hath not believed in the name of the only begotten Son of God."

4. *Failure to do good is sin.* This is the sin of omission. James 4:17: "Therefore to him that knoweth to do good, and doeth it not, to him it is sin." That is one reason I say you are sinning when, as a Christian, you don't line up with

a church where you live and serve God as a faithful Christian and church member. You say you have been saved, that you are a child of God. Now you know it's a good thing for a Christian to be lined up with His Church, the only institution Christ founded and put on the earth. If you don't do this good thing, you are committing the sin of omission. If everybody did that we would have no local churches to bring us the message of salvation.

Several years ago an explosion destroyed a school building in New London, Texas. Scores of children were killed. An investigation was made and it was found that a man who had been employed in the construction of the building knew that a faulty gas line had been installed, but he had not reported it to the authorities. He knew what he should have done, but he didn't do it. Consequently he sinned against these children and their families.

A missionary in a foreign country saw a boat capsize and saw two men thrown into the water. She was unable to swim so she called upon some men who were standing nearby to go to the rescue of the men in the water. They asked her how much she would pay them for this service, and while they quibbled over the price the two men drowned. The quibbling men were guilty of the sin of omission.

In our list of sins we must name the sin of a bad disposition. If you have malice or hatred or envy or jealousy toward anyone on earth you are guilty of sin. Christ's attitude of love and forgiveness must be ours or we are guilty of a sin which leads to many other sins.

II. Where Did Sin Come From?

Sin originated in the mind and heart of Satan. Having one of the highest positions in heaven he became puffed up with pride and sought to throw God off His throne (Isaiah 14:12-15). As a result of his rebellion Satan and his angels were cast out of heaven. Therefore we can say that Satan is the author of sin. John tells us that Satan was a sinner from the beginning (I John 3:8). Jesus tells us that

The World's Worst Disease 73

Satan is the father of lies (John 8:44). The reason we sin is because we have some of the devil in us.

In the Garden of Eden the devil tempted Adam and Eve. They fell into sin and sin entered into the bloodstream of the human race. Now it is hereditary. It passes down from one generation to the next. We are all born in sin. But it all started with Satan and the more we follow him the more we sin.

III. Who Commits Sin?

All the world stands guilty before God. "For there is not a just man upon earth, that doeth good, and sinneth not" (Ecclesiastes 7:20).

God says that there is no difference in men. Some sinners can neither read nor write, while others with university degrees often sin even more grievously. The rich man sins and the poor man sins. The bad man sins and the good man sins. The prisoner sins and the preacher sins. The pauper sins and the pope sins. "All have sinned, and come short of the glory of God" (Romans 3:23).

An American soldier in Japan was talking to a high-born Japanese lady. He brought out the fact that all of us had sinned against God. The woman became highly indignant. She said, "That may be true of Chinese or Koreans or even some Japanese, but it certainly doesn't apply to me." But God's Word says that she was wrong.

A certain judge was trying a boy for raiding a watermelon patch. He said to the boy, "Do you have anything to say for yourself?" Then the boy said, "Judge, did you ever steal a watermelon when you were a boy?" The judge promptly rapped his gavel and said, "Case dismissed." He knew that he was just as guilty as the boy was. Yes, we are all guilty.

IV. What Does Sin Do?

1. *Sin seduces.* As the spider lures the fly, so does sin lure us on to destruction. The young man who takes a drink to be sociable never intends to be a drunkard, but sin leads him on and ruins him. The man who takes ten dollars from

the company cash register intends to replace it, but sin leads him on, he becomes an embezzler and lands in prison.

The scientists tell us that one speck of dust in the control instrument can throw a giant plane off its course. They say that lint from a man's clothing can make a guided missile miss its mark. And our little sins can throw us off the track of righteousness and cause our downfall.

2. *Sin saddens.* All the sadness in the world today was brought about by sin. I have known mothers who were in good health suddenly begin to go down because of the sins of their sons. I have seen happy homes become places of misery because of the sin of one of its members.

Years ago I had sweet fellowship with one of the finest couples I had ever known. They had a happy home and two delightful children. He was the church treasurer. The entire family was dedicated and active. He was a highly respected citizen in the community. For some years I lost contact with them. Then I learned recently that he was several thousand dollars short in his position with a very reputable firm. Now he is getting up in years. He has no job and can't get one. He has lost out in every way. As he looks back on life his heart is filled with regret and sorrow. Yes, sin saddens.

I am thinking of another couple who had a teen-aged boy. These parents were very critical, they were always condemning and criticizing their pastor and church in the presence of their son. Of course, this made the boy lose all taste for Christianity and the church and he soon drifted away from all spiritual things. One night my phone rang around midnight and the sad message came that this son had been killed in an automobile accident, while under the influence of alcohol. The parents' hearts were broken. They realized that their own sin had brought his sadness upon them.

3. *Sin leaves a scar.* You may sin, later on repent of that sin, and find forgiveness, but it does something to you. David sinned greatly and sincerely repented of it. God forgave him, but his sin left a scar on his life and a tragic memory in his heart. I am sure that often in the night, when he

The World's Worst Disease

couldn't sleep, he said to himself in sorrow, "Oh, how I wish I hadn't sinned as I did." Sin leaves a scar that nothing can erase.

4. *Sin separates.* Go with me on a moonlit night to a field just outside of the city of Jerusalem. What is that object there on the ground? Why, it's a man. That man has hanged himself, the rope has broken and he has fallen to the ground. Strike a match and let's look at his face. Who is it? It's Judas, one of the disciples of the Lord Jesus. Why is he here? Why isn't he with the other disciples? And the answer is, sin. Sin separates.

Not only does sin separate here, it separates hereafter. A man boldly told a Christian worker that he intended to go to hell when he died, because his father was there and he wanted to be with him. But he didn't realize that there would be no love between a father and son in hell, only hatred and bitterness.

One who sins his life away, who leaves Jesus Christ out of his life, will be separated throughout eternity from God and all that's good and all that brings happiness.

IV. WHAT IS THE REMEDY FOR SIN?

Christ is the only Remedy. He came to die that our sins through Him might be forgiven. He was indeed "the Lamb of God, slain from the foundation of the world." If you will come to Him, He will take away your sin and give you eternal life.

A man recently said, "I don't go to church anymore. Things are changing so rapidly that you can't be sure of anything any more." Oh yes, there are two things you can always be sure of. You can be sure of the fact of sin and of the fact that Christ will save you if you come to Him.

Just suppose that you were desperately ill and the doctor came to examine you. After a thorough examination he would say, "Your condition is critical, but I have some medicine that will cure you. I will leave the medicine with you. If you don't take it, you will be dead in twenty-four hours." What would you say? Would you say, "I'll consider the matter?" Would you say, "I'll take the medicine next week?" No, no! You would say, "Give me the medicine right now, this is too important a matter for me to put off." Well, sinner friend, God has diagnosed your case. He says that you are sick with a dreadful, killing, damning disease. But He offers you a remedy in Jesus Christ. Don't delay to accept the remedy. Come to Him and say, "I know that I am a sinner. I know that I need you, please save me right now." And as sure as there is a God, so surely will He save you.

A recent news article told of the death of a certain woman. After her death they found all the medicine her doctor had prescribed for her on the shelves in her home. She had never opened a single bottle, she had never taken one dose of the medicine. She had bought it and paid for it, but she neglected the one thing that would have given her life.

On Calvary's cross the Lord Jesus paid for your salvation. If you turn your back on His gift of eternal life, if you neglect to accept the remedy for sin, there is nothing left for you but eternal death.

Bishop Joseph Barry was on a train, traveling from Los Angeles. He felt that he ought to speak to someone about Christ. He asked the porter if there were any sick people on the train. The porter told him that a young man was sick in one of the pullman berths. The bishop went to see the sick boy, a young man about twenty years of age. He could see that the boy was critically ill. He told him a few funny stories and tried to cheer him up. Then he felt sure that as a Christian he ought to do more, so he said to the boy, "I know you are lonely, but let me tell you of a Friend who will never leave you if you'll let Him come into your heart." Then he preached Jesus to him. The boy listened with great eagerness. Then the bishop offered a prayer and soon he knew Christ had become precious to the boy.

The next morning the bishop came back, parted the curtains and said to the boy, "Is everything all right this morning?" "Yes sir," the boy answered. "When you left here last night Jesus was with me and He has been here all night.

I am glad you came back so I could tell you that it is all well between me and the Lord this morning and I know it will be well with me forever."

Oh, friend without Christ, it is not well with you if you haven't found the remedy for sin. You may drop into hell at any minute. But if you will come to Jesus, it will surely be well with you forever.

8

WHEN LIFE REALLY BEGINS

John 3:1-8

Some years ago an American author gave us the expression, "Life begins at forty." Let me say to you that life begins when you are born again, when the Lord Jesus comes into your heart. A man eighty years of age was gloriously saved. A few years later one of his grandchildren said, "Granddad, how old are you?" And the old man answered, "I am just four years old." "Oh, granddad," said the little boy, "you're an old man. You are more than four years old." And he replied, "No, I am just four years of age. Eighty years I spent in the service of Satan. I have been serving God only four years. I didn't really and truly begin to live until I found Christ as my personal Saviour."

Ask Paul when he began to live and he will tell you it was when he met Christ on the Damascus Road. Ask Peter and he will tell you life really began for him when Andrew brought him to Christ. Ask Bartimaeus and he will tell you it began for him when he left his beggar's position by the side of the road, and came to Jesus. Ask the thief who died on the cross and he will say, "Life really began for me just before I died. It began when Jesus said, 'This day shalt thou be with me in paradise.'" Ask the hosts of redeemed saints in heaven and they will say, "We were sinners. We were bound for hell. But the Holy Spirit convicted us and pointed us to the Saviour. Life began when we took Him into our hearts and now we have a life that will never end."

When Life Really Begins

What is life? Is it life to live a few years, to suffer all the trials of life, to die in agony, to be covered up with six feet of earth, never to see the light again? Is that life? No, it is life to know Christ, to walk with Him on this earth and then someday to go with Him beyond the skies to a land where we'll never grow old and where sorrows never come.

In the text we see Nicodemus coming to Jesus by night. There have been many guesses as to why he came at night. Some people condemn him for coming under the cover of darkness, but we should commend him just for coming, for out of his conference with Jesus, we receive the tremendous truth about the new birth. He came to the right One, the One who has the answer to all of life's questions. He didn't go to the high priest nor to the disciples, he went to headquarters, he went to Jesus. He went to the only One who can save from sin, who can disperse the darkness and bring light and life, who can wipe away all tears and give us the gladness and joy of eternal salvation.

Now Jesus had time to talk to this hungry-hearted man. He loves sinners and always has time for them. He says, "Him that cometh to me, I will in no wise cast out" (John 6:3). He had time for the woman at the well, He had time for the thief on the cross, He has time for you. If you had been the only sinner in the world, Jesus would gladly have come down to endure all the agonies of Calvary just for you.

He sits at the right hand of God today, but if He were to look down and see one soul for whom He did not die, He would gladly lay aside the scepter and the crown and the royal robes and come down to endure again the agonies of Calvary for that one soul. Oh, what a Saviour!

Let us look at:
    I. The Man Who Needed the New Birth
   II. The Meaning of the New Birth
  III. The Method of Obtaining the New Birth

I. The Man Who Needed the New Birth

1. *Nicodemus was an intelligent man.* Jesus called him "a master of Israel." He had a master's degree in Jewish re-

ligious knowledge. He was a scholar, a religious zealot, a member of the Sanhedrin. *But he was lost.* Today the world is filled with such men. They are educated, cultured, refined, talented, but they are lost. They have never experienced the new birth. When I read something about some prominent man the thought comes to me, "Does he know Jesus Christ?" Many of them are living for this world only.

The average man is intelligent about worldly things but ignorant of spiritual matters. He can talk politics, current events, sports, but knows very little about real religion. Oh, I would rather be unlearned, live in a hut and dine on scraps, and know Christ and have a hope of heaven, than to be the most brilliant man on earth who is lost and headed for hell. Yes, Nicodemus was an intelligent man.

2. *Nicodemus was a rich man.* Jesus said that it was hard for a rich man to get to heaven. He did not say it was impossible. However, many of them are so engrossed in financial and material affairs that they have no time for God and spiritual matters. One day I visited a very rich man who was ill. When I told him I was sorry he was sick, he said, "Oh, it's nothing that money won't cure." But his money didn't save him. He died.

In the case of many men, you touch a tender and sensitive spot when you touch their money. This was true of the rich young ruler who came to Jesus. He loved his money too much to give it up and inherit eternal life. Sam Jones, the great Methodist evangelist, said it would be hard for a man to go to heaven from a three-story house. He was simply saying in a different way what Jesus said so long ago. Yes, Nicodemus was a rich man.

3. *Nicodemus was a good moral man.* He had to be a clean man to get into the Sanhedrin. The Pharisees were very strict as to morality and religious observances. They would walk only a certain distance on the Sabbath and they refused to eat an egg laid on that holy day. But morality is not enough to save a man, yet many men are depending on it. They say, "I live a good life, I am clean morally, I pay my debts, I never harm anybody." Now if a man could be saved

that way, it would not have been necessary for Jesus to go to the cross. Oh, why can't men see that salvation is only through the precious blood of the Lamb?

The moral man says, "I treat my fellow man rightly." Yes, but how have you treated Christ? You had sinned, you had rebelled against God, you were lost. But He loved you enough to die for you, that He might purchase salvation for you. But if you have rejected Him and turned your back on His love, there can be no greater sin. No matter how nicely you treat others, you are lost if your relationship to Christ is not right. Your morality will not save you. Yes, Nicodemus was a good moral man.

4. *Nicodemus was an old man.* He asked the question, "How can a man be born when he is old?" Age doesn't matter, God can save you when you are old. Years ago a man 86 years of age began to attend the services in the church where I ministered. Often he would say to me, "I am a bad one." Always I assured him that God could save the worst of sinners. Then one night he hobbled down the aisle and confessed Christ as his personal Saviour. He became a faithful and radiant Christian and never lost an opportunity to tell people that Christ had saved him in his old age.

I may be speaking to someone who is far along in years, but who hasn't been born again. There are not many years left for you, but they can be your best ones if Christ becomes your Saviour. Someone has said, "the devil has no happy old men." But Christ can give you happiness and peace. Death is coming soon. What is your hope? Christ can save you and change you and give you real hope. Nicodemus was old and he was lost.

II. THE MEANING OF THE NEW BIRTH

Jesus parallels the new birth — the spiritual birth — with the physical birth.

1. *Birth means a beginning.* When a child is born there is a beginning, he has just begun to live. You don't expect a two-day old baby to do the things he will do later on. So

the convert is just a beginner. We don't expect as much from him as we do a man who has been a Christian 25 years.

Someone says, "I would like to be a Christian, but I am afraid I could not live up to it." Well, a Christian is not a perfect person, he is just striving to become a better person. So come to Jesus. Make a start and all the help of heaven will be yours. Come to Jesus, saying, "Nothing in my hand I bring, simply to Thy cross I cling." Come in that spirit and the gates of heaven will open to you. Your name will be written in the Lamb's Book of Life.

2. *Birth implies growth.* A baby is alive at three months of age and he is alive at thirty years of age, a baby no longer. He has experienced years of physical growth. Christians are supposed to grow spiritually, also. But so many of them never experience spiritual growth. They still act like babies. It is said that a wasp is larger at birth than at any other time. Some Christians are like that. They have been born again, but they have never grown spiritually. In fact, some of them have dwindled in spiritual size.

Nourishment is necessary to growth, physical or spiritual. This spiritual growth is brought about by a study of God's Word, prayer and communion with God, church attendance, giving to the Lord, witnessing, spiritual exercise in service. Tie your arm to your side and leave it there and you'll lose the use of it. Let your talents hang idly by your side and they will atrophy, they will dry up. Get busy for God and you'll grow in grace.

3. *Birth implies a relationship.* When a child is born he has a mother and father, brothers and sisters, aunts and uncles and cousins. He has these blood connections. And as soon as a person is born again he has some new relationships. He has God as His Father, a relationship the unsaved man does not have. He has Jesus Christ as his Older Brother, ready always to help him, saying, "Lo, I'll be with you always." Then he has a multitude of brothers and sisters in Christ and the fellowship of the church.

A dear woman who could speak Spanish only, asked, "Did Jesus speak Spanish when He was here on earth?" When

When Life Really Begins

told He did not, she said, "But He certainly speaks it now. This is the only language I understand and I understand Him as He speaks to me and I'm sure He hears me when I speak Spanish to Him in prayer."

Yes, the one who has been born again has a new Father, even God, a blessed Saviour, Jesus, and a host of brothers and sisters in a great spiritual family.

4. *Birth implies a home.* Most babies are born in a hospital. Then what a day it is when the mother and baby come home! The young father is most careful as he carries the baby to the car and most tender as he carries the baby up the steps into its home. The new baby is not a foundling, he has a home. If you have been born of the Spirit, you have two homes, one on the earth and one beyond the skies.

The church is the earthly home of the believer. Jesus placed it here in the world for your instruction and inspiration and fellowship and service. If you say you can live as good outside the church as you can in it, you are simply saying that Christ made a mistake in founding the church. You ought to love the church, be jealous of its reputation, pray for it and support its work.

And then beyond this life Christ has prepared for you a heavenly home. He said, "Let not your heart be troubled: . . . In my Father's house are many mansions: . . . I go to prepare a place for you. And if I go and prepare a place for you, I will come again, and receive you unto myself; that where I am, there ye may be also" (John 14:1-3).

The church is the Christian's home for time, heaven is the Christian's home for eternity. When you are born again a mansion is set aside for you. You may sin often, you may sometimes go astray, but if you have been really saved, if you are a child of God, your name is still on the door of your mansion beyond the blue.

III. THE METHOD OF OBTAINING THE NEW BIRTH

Physical birth requires the fusing of two elements. It is the same with the spiritual birth. Two things must come together, repentance and faith. Come to Jesus, repenting of your sin and trusting Him as your Saviour. In that minute you will receive the new birth, you will have a new nature, a new life, a new hope, a home in heaven reserved for you.

Many years ago a young preacher in England pitched his tent in a neglected area where there was no church and preached the saving gospel each night to the crowds that attended. Among the converts was a fourteen-year-old boy whose mother was dead and whose father was a saloon-keeper. After his conversion the boy pled with his father to attend the services with him, but his father cursed him and told him to forget it. On Saturday night the boy rose up in the meeting and said, "Please pray for my daddy. He is a saloon-keeper and I want so much for him to be saved."

On Monday someone told this man that his son had requested prayer for him in the meeting. It made him furious. When the boy came home from school his father jerked him up and said, "If you want to be a Christian, go ahead. But leave my name out of it. Don't talk about me." The boy made this promise, but again on Saturday night his heart was breaking for his father, so he stood up again and asked for prayer for his father. Again someone told the father about this, hoping that this would touch and convict him. When the boy came in from school, the man took a strap and beat the boy until the blood stained his shirt. The boy soon fainted and fell on the floor. The cruel man threw a bucket of water on him, kicked him and went on to the saloon. The boy stumbled to his knees, climbed into bed and sobbed himself to sleep.

That night the father, feeling sorry for the way he had treated the boy, slipped into his room. He found the boy with tears coursing down his cheeks and his shirt stiff with blood. He fell on his knees and placed his arm across the boy. The boy shrank back in fear, but his father said, "Son, I am sorry for what I did. I'll never do it again." He began to cry as he pulled the boy to him. He said, "Son, are you really a Christian?" The boy replied, "Yes, daddy." "Can you pray, son?" the father asked. "Yes, sir," replied the boy, "I have learned to pray a little." "Well," said the man, "after all I've done, can you pray for me?" "I surely will," said the boy.

Both of them got down on their knees and the father tenderly rested his arm around the boy's bleeding back. Then the boy prayed, "Dear Lord, save my daddy. I want him to be a Christian." The man began to sob, then he said, "Son, tell me how to become a Christian." The boy explained to him about repentance and faith and the father said, "I'll do that right now. I am sorry for all my sins. I am trusting Christ with all my heart."

The next morning the father shaved and put on his best Sunday suit. To the boy he said, "I don't want you to go to school this morning. I'll write the teacher a note." After breakfast the father said, "I want you to take me to that preacher." The boy said, "You're not going to fight him, are you?" "No, son, I'll never do anything like that again," he answered. They went to see the preacher, the boy and his father told their story and soon the man was again confessing his faith in Christ. "Preacher, come with me," said the father. They went down to the saloon and he took an axe, demolished the bar and broke every bottle of whiskey in the house. Then he handed the keys of the building to the preacher, saying, "It's all yours now. Use it in any way you please." Now that building houses a church and the former saloon-keeper is an officer in that church.

Why did it all happen? Because the man had been born again and Christ had changed his life. You may not be as sinful as that man was, but without Christ you are just as lost as he was. But Christ is still in the life-changing business. Come to Him. Be born again. Then life will really begin for you.

9

"REVIVE US AGAIN"

Isaiah 1:1-18

As I come to think of a revival my mind goes back to the first revival I ever held. When God called me to preach, I was living in Atlanta, was married and the father of one little boy. I had finished only two years of high school and was trying to make my way in the business world. My call to preach was as clear as the sunlight. It involved a tremendous spiritual and emotional experience.

Two preachers in the city gave me the opportunity to preach my first sermons. Then I was invited to preach three Sundays in a small church on the edge of the city. The next week that church called me as their pastor. When I had been there just a few weeks the deacons said to me, "We need a revival and we want you to do the preaching." I consented to do so but I was literally "scared to death." I had no sermons ahead, I had very little experience in preaching, it was my first revival.

I preached every night for two weeks. During the daytime I would study and work and pray as I prepared my sermon. That night I would pour out my heart as I told them everything I had learned that day. But oh, how God did bless. Eighty new members were added to the church, the majority of them coming on a confession of their faith.

But the revival went even deeper than that. Church members got right with each other and with God. Even in the cottage prayer meetings people cried out for mercy and asked for prayer. The success of the meeting came not because of the green young preacher or his hard worked-out sermons, but because the Holy Spirit took over and did His mighty work. I wish I could experience more real revivals like that first one.

In this text from Isaiah God is speaking out about the sins of Israel. They have rebelled against Him, they have forsaken Him, they have provoked Him to anger with their sin and idolatry. Oh, they went to church all right and went through their religious ceremonies, but this did nothing for them in the matter of true worship. They went through the form but their hearts were not in it and God knew it. So He said, "I'm sick and tired of all this, away with it." And then the gracious Lord issued this loving invitation, "Come now, and let us reason together, saith the Lord; though your sins be as scarlet, they shall be as white as snow; though they be red like crimson, they shall be as wool" (v. 18).

Now that is just like God. Although we break His heart with our sins, He stretches out His arms to us and invites us to come to Him for forgiveness and cleansing.

The conditions of this day are very much like the conditions of that day. People fill the church on Sunday morning when it is convenient and go through the forms of religion. A few of them come back on Sunday night and on Wednesday night. But so many hearts are far from God. We need a spiritual revolution. We need something to wake us up to our cold backslidden condition and bring us back to a warm-hearted love for Christ.

I. We Need a Revival Now

Now, what is a revival? It is an awakening of God's people which causes them to become active for God. It is something that must happen in the hearts of Christians, then it will reach out to touch the unsaved for Christ. Oh, if all Christians were what they ought to be, we would not have to worry about winning the lost to Christ. They would see such a difference in us that they would cry out for the same thing that has changed us.

Let us look at some of the things that engulf Christians today and that hold back a real revival.

1. *First, there is worldliness.* What is worldliness? It is anything of the world that we put above the things of God. The world is pressing in on us today. Every worldly organization clamors for us and our services, promising us great rewards of prestige and position. And too many of our people are responding to these calls. They are virtually saying, "This is it. This means more than the service of Christ."

I have seen scores of people who were once active for the Lord and in His Church, but who are now giving all their time and energy and influence to worldly things. They begin by saying, "I have too much to do, so I'll give up some of my church work." They never say, "I am too busy with the world, I must give up some of it so I can give more time to the Lord's work."

I realize that there are many things in the world that are not bad in themselves. But it's wrong if you let even good things come between you and the Lord's work. Some people go after worldly things, thinking that these things will add joy to their lives. But the Bible says, "Seek ye first the kingdom of God, and his righteousness; and all these things shall be added unto you" (Matthew 6:33).

One afternoon I was making some pastoral calls and dropped in on one of my members who had not been attending church. "Pastor," she said, "I'm sorry I can't come to church, but my eight-year-old boy is not in good health and I cannot take him out." A little later I was called upon to help a charitable organization in one of its projects. I went down several nights and stayed until nearly midnight. And there was that woman, with her boy by her side, every night. People think preachers are fools. They make their excuses for not serving God, when all the time the preachers know these excuses are only lies. The whole truth is that they love the world more than they love the Lord.

There's one reason we need revival. We need to get such a fresh glimpse of Christ and such a disgusting look at ourselves that we cry out, "Lord, I'm through with petty, worldly things. From now on I'll put Thee first in my life."

2. *Next, there is indifference.* This is the thing that engulfs so many church members. When they were first converted they couldn't get enough of Christ. They could hardly wait for Sunday to come. They wanted every contact that they could have with the Lord and His people. But as time went by they lost their zest for spiritual things. Now they say, "It doesn't matter. They can get along in the church without me." Maybe so, but can you get along without these things of the Spirit?

Do you sit at home on Sunday night and watch television? If so, you are simply saying, "I don't care whether or not they have a service, I don't care whether or not souls are saved. Christ has saved me and will take me to heaven someday. I don't care about anything else." Is that your attitude? Oh, you don't voice that feeling audibly, but that's your attitude, nevertheless. Oh, how we do need a soul-shaking revival among our church members.

I remember how President Kennedy was once criticized severely for having a cocktail party in the White House on Sunday night. The criticism was justified, whether the party was on Sunday night or any other night. But I couldn't help but wonder at the time if those same critics were as loyal to Christ and His teachings as they should be. It's so easy to see the other fellow's sin and to overlook our own.

Two preachers were talking at a convention. One of them said, "We have quit having a Wednesday night prayer meeting in our church." His friend asked, "How do your deacons feel about it?" And the other preacher replied, "Oh, they haven't found out about it yet." And many of our people are just that indifferent.

3. *Next, there is sin.* The moral standards of America are lower than ever. Anything goes in this age of the "new morality" as long as you can get away with it. There was a time when no profanity was allowed in the newspapers, over radio or television, or in the movies. How times have changed! All of these media are filled with profanity. The Ten Com-

mandments no longer form our moral code. We go by the standards of Hollywood and the world. Forty years ago only one out of twenty-five marriages ended in divorce. Today the ratio is one out of three. Then think of the wave of sexual immorality sweeping our beloved land. Vance Havner says "it is sex o'clock in America." Sex is flagrantly displayed on every side. Nearly every product on the market is advertised by sexy looking pictures. Our magazines cater almost completely to the flesh. No wonder so many of our people, both young and old, are going to the dogs, morally.

Now it would be bad enough if these things were confined to people outside of the church. But multitudes of our church members are engulfed by the waves of sin and worldliness and neglect. No wonder the times cry out for a revival. We need it in our own hearts, among those people who are the children of the King.

II. God Gave Revival in Other Days

When it seemed that life was at its lowest ebb, God sent revival to save the day. In Elijah's time He sent a revival. Ahab and Jezebel were on the throne. They had sinned above all other rulers and had led the people astray. They had killed God's prophets. The whole nation had turned its back upon God and had gone after Baal.

In the midst of all this sin Elijah stepped forth. He challenged the prophets of Baal, eight hundred and fifty of them, to meet him in a contest on Mt. Carmel. All the day long these prophets called upon Baal to answer by fire, but nothing happened. Then when Elijah prayed God heard and answered by fire. Greatly moved, the people cried out, "The Lord, he is God." The prophets of Baal were destroyed and the people turned back to God. He had given revival (I Kings 18).

In Jonah's time God sent revival. Nineveh was filled with idolatry, the people worshiped the fish god. Then God called Jonah to go and preach repentance to the Ninevites. You know the story. The rebellious preacher ran away from God, he went toward Tarshish instead of Nineveh. But God sent a storm after him and a great fish to rescue him. In the close quarters of the fish's belly Jonah repented and promised God that he would do His bidding. The fish spat Jonah out on the shore and he hit the beach running, running toward Nineveh. There his sermon theme was, "Repent or perish." God used that kind of preaching then as He does now. The whole city, led by the king, repented and turned back to God. He had given revival.

In Jesus' day God sent revival. One day our Lord sat on the well curb just outside the city of Sychar, while His disciples went into the city to buy food. (See John 4.) And a woman came to the well, a woman who was a deep-dyed sinner. Jesus talked with her, showed her her sin and revealed Himself to her. She felt her need, repented of her sin and put her faith in the Saviour.

Now, what did she do? She went back into the city, leaving her waterpot behind. She had a glorious message to deliver. When she arrived in the city she told the people all about this wonderful Saviour who had forgiven and saved her. Then the whole city came out to meet Jesus and many of them believed on Him. God had sent revival.

On the day of Pentecost God sent revival (Acts 2). Jerusalem was Gospel-hardened. John the Baptist had preached there. The people listened to him and went on in their sin. Jesus preached there and performed many mighty miracles, but they hated Him and put Him to death. His disciples forsook Him and fled. One denied Him; one betrayed Him and later committed suicide. Certainly all hope was gone. It would be of no use for that little group to get together and to try to have a revival.

But God intervened. Fifty days after Jesus died on the cross the Holy Spirit fell upon this little group in mighty power. Then the man who had denied Jesus stood up and preached a simple sermon and three thousand people were saved. God had sent revival.

Billy Graham went to Hollywood, the world center of sin and immorality. The spiritual life of the city was practically nil. What could an evangelist do there? Well, God used him mightily. The crowds came and thousands were saved. The meeting was extended to eight weeks. National magazines played up the meeting in pictures and stories. Billy Graham was catapulted into worldwide fame, making it possible for him to go all over the world and get a good hearing for the gospel of Christ. God had sent revival.

III. God Can Give Revival Today

God never changes. The same God who gave revivals in the olden days is just as eager to give them today. But we must pay the price for revival. We can't sit idly by and just expect a great revival to take place. We must pay the price. A revival doesn't start five miles away and then come into the church. The reverse is true. A true revival must begin with the people of God.

First, we must realize our own needs. You can say, "Oh, preacher, I'm all right. I live a pretty good life. I am a faithful church member. There's nothing wrong with me." But you can't truthfully say that to God. You can't tell God that it is all well with your soul. Let me give you a good exercise. Take a piece of paper and write down all the things you do which are not becoming to a consecrated Christian. Then write down all the things you ought to do as an obedient Christian and which you don't do. You will find that your average is pretty low. Then take that paper before God and say, "Lord, help me to get these wrong things out of my life and help me to do all the things I have failed to do." Then you will be on the road to real revival, as far as your own personal life is concerned.

Next we must adopt God's recipe for revival. We find it in II Chronicles 7:14: "If my people, which are called by my name, shall humble themselves, and pray, and seek my face, and turn from their wicked ways; then will I hear from heaven, and will forgive their sin, and will heal their land."

Are you one of God's people? His people are those who have been born again through a vital saving experience with Jesus Christ. Revival must come through His people. Bartenders never bring revival. Gamblers and thieves never bring revival. It must come through God's people.

Then we are to humble ourselves. That isn't easy for the average American. But if we want God's blessings we must humble ourselves before Him, we must become as nothing. Arrogant, boastful people never make any connection with God. Do we really have anything to be proud of? Oh, how sinful, how unfaithful, how fruitless we have been! We fall so very short of what God wants us to be. We need to cry out, "Lord, I am a sinful person. I am not worthy of the least of thy mercies." The lower we get in our own estimation, the higher we can get with God.

> Alas and did my Saviour bleed,
> And did my Sovereign die,
> Would He devote that sacred head
> For such a worm as I?
> — *Isaac Watts*

Teddy Roosevelt would not sing that song that way. He said that he was not a "worm." And some of our modern hymnbooks have changed the words. But the Bible says we are just "worms." And we never get up to God until we get down in humility.

Then we must pray. Oh, how many church members are out of touch with God, simply because they do not pray. A certain man spent a week in the hospital. No one in his church knew about his illness. Later he said, "I was in the hospital a week and no one came to see me." Now his pastor and the church staff were available and ready to visit him, but he didn't call on them. And God is ready to hear and forgive your sins, but you must call on Him. What a real revival would be ours if every one of us fell on our knees and prayed for God to send a revival into our own souls!

Then we must seek God's face, and turn from our wicked ways. Put these two things together. If you seek God's face you will turn from your wicked ways. When Isaiah saw God high and lifted up, then he recognized his own sinfulness and cried out for forgiveness.

This is God's message for your heart. So go and get alone with God. Humble yourself, confess your sins, ask Him to forgive you and send a revival to your soul. His promises are always good. He promises to hear your prayer and forgive your sins.

A certain evangelist was holding a meeting in one of our churches. One day he and the pastor visited in a home for the purpose of talking to a man who was unsaved. That man's wife was a member of this particular church. After giving this unsaved man the Bible plan of salvation, the preacher said, "Let's kneel in prayer." After the prayer the man was given an opportunity to accept Christ, but he declined. Again the preacher read the Bible and prayed, but the man shook his head and said, "Not now, some other time."

Then a strange thing happened. The lost man's wife fell upon her knees, put her hands over her face and began to pray out loud. She confessed her own unfaithfulness to Christ and how she had gone with her husband to the wrong places and had done the wrong things. She confessed to God how her own life had made it hard for her husband to see his need of Christ. When she had finished her prayer, tears were streaming down her husband's face. "Will you here and now accept Christ as your Saviour?" the preacher asked the man. He said that he would. He made his public profession of his faith, was baptized and joined the church with his wife. Now they are living good lives for the Lord.

Don't you see the answer? When Christians get right with God, things begin to happen. Revival comes, souls are saved, lives are blessed, churches are revived. So let us pray in the words of the old song, "O Lord, send a revival and let it begin in me."

10

THE FOUR-SQUARE GOSPEL

I Corinthians 15:1-4

Sometime ago I had the privilege of going through beautiful Forest Lawn Cemetery in Los Angeles. Among the more expensive tombstones I saw one about twenty feet in length. As I came closer I saw the name on it, the name of "Aimee Semple McPherson." Then I remembered that brilliant, controversial woman preacher who preached in that city and around the world. She was very dramatic and drew large congregations. She preached salvation by grace and I am sure many were saved under her ministry. She called her gospel the "four-square gospel."

I do not know what she meant by "the four-square gospel," but I know what I mean. There are four sides to the Gospel of Christ. This makes it a complete, a finished Gospel. We need add nothing nor subtract anything from it. There are four sides to a square, there are four sides to the Gospel. It is not complete otherwise.

It is the Gospel Christ died to give us. It is the Gospel preached by Peter and Paul. It is the Gospel preached by the mighty preachers of all ages. It is the Gospel I've tried to proclaim over the years. This is the only Gospel the true preacher has, the only one he needs, the only one that gets results. You can preach a watered-down gospel and no one will be blessed, no one will be saved. We must preach the Gospel given us in the New Testament. Let us look at the four sides of this Gospel.

I. The First Side of the Square — Christ Lived

I never saw Him, I never heard Him speak, I never watched Him perform His mighty miracles. But I have read about Him in the greatest and most authentic book in the world, the God-inspired Word of God, the Bible. I know He came into the world, I know He walked the dusty roads of Palestine and climbed its mountains. I know He was baptized in the historic River Jordan. I know He touched men and blessed them.

I never saw George Washington but I believe he lived. The history books tell us about him and those who knew him passed on down to us the facts of his life. I know he was born in Virginia, that he became an army general, that he fought in two wars. I know he was the first president of our country. Every school child can tell you about him.

I remember when I rode into the city of Washington for the first time. I was greatly moved. Our capital is named after him, one state is named after him, nearly every state has a town named after him. Now you don't name states and cities after men who never lived. One day I rode an elevator to the top of the Washington monument, which is 555 feet high. All over the United States there are other monuments erected to his memory. You don't erect monuments to the memory of men who never lived.

Then I rode out to Mount Vernon, Washington's beautiful home on the Potomac. The guide said, "This is where he ate, this is where he slept, this was his study." Then I walked down to the garden tomb. I looked through the iron gate at the two graves and was greatly moved as I read the inscription, "I am the resurrection and the life, he that believeth in me, though he were dead, yet shall he live."

Yes, I know George Washington lived. I have read about him in many books, I have seen where he lived and where he is buried. But how do I know Jesus lived? I know because a Book more authoritative than any man's book tells me so. It is God's book. Historians can make mistakes, but there is no mistake in the Book God wrote. That Book tells us that Jesus lived with God before the world was made. "In the beginning was the Word [Christ], and the Word was with God, and the Word was God" (John 1:1). When God said, "Let us make man in our own image," He included both the Son and the Holy Spirit along with Himself. Jesus was living in all eternity past, with the Father and the Holy Spirit.

But He not only lived in heaven, He came down to earth and lived here. God wanted Him to come down to this world, to share all of man's problems and burdens and to die for man's sin. He could have sent Him down as a full-grown man, but He wanted Him to live as a human being and go through all of our experiences, so that He could help us in our time of need.

So God planted Him in the womb of the Virgin Mary and in due time He came forth as a tiny babe. Remember that God did this, no man's seed was used. I don't know how God did it, but God said He did it and I believe it. After all, the God who made heaven and earth could do this. The God who made the human body with all its functioning parts, the most intricate machine in the world, could send His Son to the earth this way. Yes, He was born, He lived, He went through every experience of life except sin. He ate and drank, He slept, He talked, He wept, He loved.

He lived to show us what God is like. The Old Testament prophets said, "Turn from your sin, turn to God." And people asked, "What kind of a being is God, what is He like? How does He feel about us? Is He an avenging monster or is He our friend?" Well, Jesus came and said, "If you want to know what God is like, look at me. The Father and I are One. He that hath seen me hath seen the Father." And we look at Jesus and learn what God is like. The great, loving, compassionate Son tells us that the Father is also loving, compassionate, merciful, forgiving.

Jesus also came to show us how to live. We don't need a psychiatrist or philosopher to tell us how to live, we need only look to Jesus as He is revealed in the Bible. He is our example. Live like Him and your life will be what it ought to be. Oh, if we'll just live as He lived, the world will see Jesus in us and will be constrained to follow Him.

Let us go to heaven and interview just one man, Lazarus. "Lazarus, did Jesus ever live on the earth?" And Lazarus, with heaven's light on his face, answers, "Yes, He lived, He came often to our house in Bethany. My sisters and I loved Him very much. Then I was sick and they told me later that I died and was buried. But four days later Jesus came and raised me up and gave life to me again. I lived to praise Him several years after that. Yes, He lived." All heaven is filled with some who knew He lived, and there are those in hell who know it, also.

Yes, Jesus lived and He still lives. He is not dead, regardless of what some modern theologians say about Him.

II. SECOND SIDE OF THE SQUARE — CHRIST DIED

God said Christ would die hundreds of years before He came into the world. "He was wounded for our transgressions, he was bruised for our iniquities; the chastisement of our peace was upon him; and with his stripes we are healed" (Isaiah 53:5). God said He would be cut off from the land of the living, He said His grave would be among the wicked and the rich (Isaiah 53:8, 9). And what God said, literally happened. On the darkest day that ever dawned, they took Jesus out and slew Him on a Roman cross. Then He was buried in a rich man's tomb, with the wicked all around Him.

Why did He die? He died to save us from our sin. He died not as a martyr, but as a Saviour. The Bible tells us that "Christ died for our sins according to the scriptures" (I Corinthians 15:3). The Bible tells us that "God so loved the world, that he gave his only begotten Son" (John 3:16). The Bible tells us that "as Moses lifted up the serpent in the wilderness, even so must the Son of man be lifted up" (John 3:14).

Jesus is not only our example, our teacher, our friend, He is our Saviour. Others can set an example for us, others can teach us, others can be our friends. But only Jesus can be our Saviour.

The Four-Square Gospel

A few years ago two ammunition ships exploded off the coast of California. More than 300 people died within a few seconds of time. Flames shot high in the air. Windows were shaken out in San Francisco, thirty miles away. But facing the water was a little Christian mission where Christians met to worship and praise God. On the building was an electric sign with two words on it, "Jesus Saves." The little building was practically demolished but above the ruins and the debris the sign was still working and sending out its message to the world. Yes, the world may tumble down around us, but that glorious truth still remains, "Jesus Saves." That is why He died, to save us.

Do your sins vex and condemn you? Bring them to the cross. All the way through the Bible, God is issuing His loving invitation to you. He wants you to come unto Him that He might wash away your sins.

Bruce, the king of Scotland, once fled before his enemies. He left his castle and plunged into a deep forest. But soon he heard the baying of his own blood-hounds. His enemies had come to the castle and set them upon his trail. He knew that they would soon overtake him. Then he came to a swiftly-flowing stream, plunged into the water and walked downstream for several miles. The dogs lost his trail at the edge of the stream and he was safe. It's the same way with our sins. We try to evade them and the guilt they bring, but they come baying at our heels. Is there any relief? Yes.

> There is a fountain filled with blood,
> Drawn from Immanuel's veins,
> And sinners plunged beneath that flood,
> Lose all their guilty stains.
> — *William Cowper*

Do you want to go to heaven at the end of the way? Of course you do, if you are a sensible person. Well, there's only one way and that's by the way of the cross. "Neither is there salvation in any other: for there is none other name under heaven given among men, whereby we must be saved" (Acts 4:12).

Oh, my friends, uncertain, unsettled, unhappy, unsaved, come to the cross. Leave all your sins there, put them upon Him who is eager to bear them for you. Today He opens wide His arms and says to you, "Come unto me, all ye that labour and are heavy laden, and I will give you rest" (Matthew 11:28).

III. Third Side of the Square — Christ Arose From the Grave

At three o'clock in the afternoon, Jesus bowed His lovely head and died. Oh, what a sight! The angels of heaven must have wept as they saw the Son of God hanging there. God's heart must have broken. Even those around the cross, the soldiers, said, "We've never seen a man like this one. He must have been the Son of God."

Now Jesus had two secret disciples, a rich man named Joseph of Arimathea and the Jewish leader who had come to Him by night, Nicodemus. They came and asked Pilate for permission to bury the Saviour's body, and this permission was granted. They tenderly lifted the body down, wrapped it in grave clothes and placed it in Joseph's new tomb. Then they turned away and went sadly home. The emptiest feeling on earth comes when one turns away from a freshly made grave, with the realization that one will never see that loved one again in this world.

Now Christ had told the disciples over and over that He would rise up from the dead, but the idea went right over their heads. It was unthinkable that a man would breathe his last breath and then come back to live again, so the disciples put the thought entirely out of their minds. Christ was dead. He had raised others, but no one could raise Him. So with Him they buried all their hopes and dreams. Surely the hours that followed must have been filled with the heaviest sorrow and deepest grief.

Oh, ye of little faith, Peter, James, John and all the others, don't you know that no grave can contain Him? He is not only the Lord of Life, He is the King of Death. Death can hold you and me, but not Jesus. He slept peacefully until

Sunday morning. His tired, broken body needed rest. Then He arose, took off the grave clothes, folded the napkin that had been about His head and laid it aside. Then He walked back into life.

> Low in the grave He lay,
>   Jesus my Saviour,
> Waiting the coming day,
>   Jesus my Lord;
>
> Up from the grave He arose,
> With a mighty triumph o'er His foes,
> He arose a victor from the dark domain,
> And He lives forever with the saints to reign,
> He arose! He arose!
> Hallelujah, Christ arose!
>
> *— Robert Lowry*

Is this Christ real to you or is He just a man who lived and died and is now gone? Dr. R. W. Dale, the great English preacher, was preparing his Easter sermon. He was going to tell his people about the resurrection. Up until this time it was just something that he had read about in the Bible. But as he meditated on the matter, suddenly something happened. The room seemed to be filled with the presence of Christ and the preacher felt that presence as never before. He walked up and down his study, saying, "He is really alive. I know it and I'll tell my people so." And from that hour there was a new note of victory in his ministry.

I am afraid that many of us live poor, half-hearted, faltering lives because Christ is not real to us. He is some far-off being who is almost non-existent. But let me tell you that He came out of that grave to walk by our sides. He came to save, He came to comfort, He came to guide, He came to bless. Oh, how we do need to discover anew a living Saviour. And we can find Him if we will throw out of our lives those things which displease Him and seek a closer walk with Him.

Now because He lives we can live also. Death is not the end, it is a glorious beginning. I could go today to a cemetery in a small North Georgia town where my mother and father are buried and as I stood by their graves I could say,

"Is this all? This six feet of earth, these ashes. Is this all that is left of them?" And from beyond the tomb I could hear a voice saying, "I am the resurrection and the life, these loved ones live again. This mortal has put on immortality and this corruptible has put on incorruption." Then I know that because Christ lives, they, too, live again.

The Romans had thirty names for death and there is no hope in any of them. They called death "a mower with a sickle, a hunter with his traps, a demon with a cup of poison, a jailer with his keys, an iron slumber, a shattered pillar, a crushed flower with the fragrance gone, a broken harp with all the music gone." But the Bible calls death a "sleep." We go to sleep in Jesus and we wake up in glory. We feel the touch of a loving hand and find it is God's hand. We breathe new air and find it is celestial air, we land in a new country and find it heaven.

For the Christian death is just a translation from an unfriendly world to a world where our Best Friend awaits us. It is just a carriage that takes us from a land of sorrow and heartbreak to a land where God wipes away every tear.

Many people say, "I want to see my boy, my mother, my father, my husband, my wife." Well, we can see them if we love the Lord Jesus Christ. But when we get there I believe we will want to see Him first of all. We'll want to fall at His feet and thank Him for saving us and bringing us safely home.

IV. Fourth Side of the Square — Christ Is Coming Again

His coming again will complete our salvation which began when we received Him as our Saviour. Paul said that he would not have us to be ignorant concerning this important matter. And it is mentioned 318 times in the New Testament. One out of every twenty-five verses speaks of it. This great truth leaps out at us from nearly every page of the New Testament. Let us think of those things that will happen when He comes.

First, when He comes He will take up two groups to be

with Himself. He will raise up the bodies of all who died in Christ, making them over into His own glorious likeness. Then He will catch up all living Christians, transforming them as they rise up to meet Him. From that moment on all believers will be with Him forever and be like Him forever, in every way.

Then, the tribulation period will engulf this earth, bringing suffering, sorrow and despair. It will be a horrible time, but remember that all Christians will be up in heaven with Christ.

Then Christ will come back to earth with all of His saints. He will reign upon the earth in a perfect period of a thousand years. Then He will punish Satan and his followers, casting them into the lake of fire. When all this is accomplished, then the eternal ages will begin, with Christ and His people in a heaven of bliss, and Satan and his followers in a hell of eternal punishment.

His coming in the air could happen at any minute. All that the Bible tells us that must happen before He returns has already happened, every prophecy has been fulfilled. At any minute the skies could open and He could return. Don't you think so? "In such an hour as ye think not, the Son of Man cometh."

Oh, if it happened now, would you be ready? Not if you are unsaved, not if you are not actively serving Him in His church and in your daily life. But for the Christian it will be a glorious hour. All of his troubles will be over, all of his tears will be wiped away, all of his problems will be solved. He will have a perfect body, he will be with Jesus and his loved ones.

A few years ago a young man was brought to a London hospital. He had been blinded by an accident in his boyhood. A gifted surgeon, believing he could restore his eyesight, performed a very delicate operation. The bandages were kept on the young man's eyes for several days. Then came the day for the bandages to be removed. It was a time of tension and excitement. Would the operation prove to be a success? Would he be able to see? His mother and father were there, his friends were there, anxious about the outcome. Finally the surgeon removed the last bandage, and he opened his eyes. Oh, wonder of wonders, he could see again! But he closed his eyes very quickly, then he said, "Doctor, stand around here in front of me. The first sight I want to see is the face of the man who gave me my sight."

Oh, don't you want to see Jesus who gave you your spiritual eyesight, who has blessed you over the years, and who is taking you to heaven? Can you say with John, "Even so, come, Lord Jesus. I am ready"?

Well, there's the four-square Gospel. Jesus lived, He died, He rose from the grave, He is coming again. I have a question for you. Is He yours? Have you trusted Him as your Saviour? Are you following Him and living for Him as your Lord?

When I came to Christ as a teen-age boy I began to pray for the salvation of my brother, George, who was several years older than I was. I talked to him about the matter, but in vain. Later, after I entered the ministry, he would come once in a while to hear me preach. After several years had gone by he came to hear me one night in a revival meeting in Atlanta. When the invitation was given he came forward to confess his faith in Christ. The pastor gave me the privilege of baptizing him.

Twenty years went by. Then one morning another brother called and said, "George died last night." His wife asked me to conduct the funeral. At that service I could say, "The greatest day in George's life was when he trusted Christ and prepared for this hour."

What will the preacher say at your funeral? Are you ready for eternity?

11

"A RENDEZVOUS WITH DEATH"

Hebrews 9:27, 28

During World War I a man wrote a poem about death. He was a soldier in active service who must have had a premonition of his own impending decease. The first line of the poem is, "I have a rendezvous with death." I believe he was killed in battle. He really had a rendezvous with death. Now if our Lord tarries we, too, have a rendezvous with death. It may come suddenly, it may come after a lingering illness, but come it will. Some of you who are here in good health may be gone in thirty days. Some who are lying low in the hospital may live for many years. Death is a mysterious thing, but it is a certain thing. Every cemetery, every funeral, every obituary notice, tell us that death is sure to come.

The funeral directors make death as beautiful as possible. They paint the lifeless face to give it a lifelike glow. They place the body in a satin-lined casket. They put beautiful flowers all around. At the cemetery they cover the clods with artificial grass. They do their best, but still death is never beautiful.

I. GOD'S WORD ABOUT DEATH

The Garden of Eden was a beautiful spot. Sin and death had never entered its portals. Then God said to Adam and Eve, "You may eat of the fruit of all the trees in the garden except one. If you eat of that tree you shall surely die." But they disobeyed God, ate of that forbidden fruit and died spiritually that moment. Then physical death set up in their bodies and the gradual process of decay began. We are familiar with that process today.

God later lists nine men from Adam to Noah. One of them, Enoch, was translated to heaven. What does the holy record say about the other eight? ". . . he died . . . he died." God is telling us that He meant what He said when He said, "Thou shalt surely die." Then read the history of the kings: "They lived. . . . They reigned. . . . They died. They lived. . . . They reigned. . . . They died." God said to Moses, "The time will come when you will die." He said to Ezekiel, "The soul that sinneth, it shall die." He sent this word to Hezekiah, "Set your house in order for you are going to die." (See Isaiah 38.)

Jesus talked often of death. He told of the beggar who died and went up to abide in Abraham's bosom. He told of the rich man who died and went to hell. (See Luke 16:19-31.) He told of the rich farmer whom God called a "fool" and who died in his sleep (Luke 12:13-21). He told the Pharisees that they would die in their sin (John 8:24).

The Bible tells of the death of great multitudes. Pharaoh and his mighty Egyptian army died in the Red Sea (Exodus 14). Sennacherib's army of 185,000 was slain by the angel of the Lord in one night (II Kings 20:35, 36). Herod killed many babies (Matthew 2). It is prophesied in the Word that millions will die in the battle of Armageddon (Revelation 16, 19). The Bible tells us that Abraham, Isaac and Jacob died, that David and Solomon died. We read in the Book that John the Baptist and Stephen met violent deaths. Paul said he was ready to be offered, he was ready for death. The fact of death is written on almost every page of the Bible.

Some years ago a certain group advertised that "millions now living shall never die." If you are living when Jesus comes in the air this will be true of you. When He comes all living Christians will be caught up to meet Him in the air. They will not taste death. Oh, how glorious to be in that number!

II. The Origin of Death

The Bible plainly tells us that death was born out of sin. The experience in Eden of which I have already spoken attests to the fact. When man first sinned, death passed on down to all of his descendants. In fact, death touches all of nature. Flowers bloom but for a few days before they die. Crops are carefully cultivated and then they die. The green leaves on the trees die. The cattle on a thousand hills die.

You and I carry death about in our bodies. The bones are getting more brittle and the teeth are decaying. The hair is turning gray or turning out. The eyes are growing weaker. Cancer is forming in some, heart muscles are weakening in others, the blood pressure is going up. Death is heading our way. During the war some men were classified as 4-F. Some of us could be classified as 5-B, "baldness, bifocals, bridgework, bulges and bunions."

Certain "divine healers" tell us that it is God's plan for all of us to have perfect health. They say that if we don't have perfect health, it is because we don't have enough faith. Yet they get sick and go to hospitals. They wear glasses and hearing aids, they go to the dentist, they die. I know that God often answers prayer and heals the sick. Yet this doesn't arrest the hand of death. We'll never have perfect bodies until Jesus comes and we rise in "His own glorious likeness." "It is appointed unto men once to die" and every day we come closer to that fateful hour.

When our boys were small and we were on a long automobile trip, we would amuse them by playing "cow poker." One of them would count the cows on one side of the car and the other one would count the ones on his side of the car as we rode along. A cow would count as one, a goat as five, and a gray horse would double the number. But when a cemetery would show up on one of the boy's side, he would lose all his points. And in real life every cemetery tells us that we are losing the game of life.

The largest part of the florists' business is furnishing flowers for the dead. The life insurance agent sells his policies by proving that men die. The white crosses along the highway speak of traffic deaths. Thousands are killed yearly in accidents of various kinds, and thousands commit suicide. In other days the architects remembered this rule, "Make all the doors and stairways large enough to admit a casket."

But you may say, "All these facts and figures don't scare me." They don't scare me either, for I have placed all my hope in One who has conquered death. But if you are not a Christian you ought to have sense enough to be scared. Death will bring an end to all of your opportunities to be saved. And remember this — death may be waiting right now to spring upon you. Your silk-lined casket may be in the funeral parlor at this moment.

III. What Happens When You Die?

1. *What happens to the Christian at death?* His body goes into the grave. That grave may be in a cemetery, it may be at the bottom of the sea, it may be on the desert sands, it may be on a mountaintop. The body decays in that grave, and this corruption remains there until Jesus comes. When He comes in the air the Christian's body is raised, it is changed and made like Jesus, it goes up to be forever with the Lord. But remember, the bodies of the unsaved dead will not be raised for another thousand years.

There is no such thing as soul-sleeping in the grave. Paul said that to be "absent from the body" was "to be present with the Lord" (II Corinthians 5:8). He also said, "For I am in a strait betwixt two, having a desire to depart, and to be with Christ; which is far better: nevertheless to abide in the flesh is more needful . . ." (Philippians 1:23, 24). He expected his soul, his spirit, his real self, to go up to be with Jesus the minute he died. If the soul sleeps, Paul, who died 1,900 years ago, has not seen Jesus yet. There is nothing in the Scriptures to warrant a belief in soul-sleeping.

When a Christian dies, his body goes into the grave, but his spirit, his soul, goes up to be with the Lord. As soon as you die in Christ, your soul takes its flight to "realms of light." Jesus said to the dying, repentant thief, "To day shalt thou be with me in paradise" (Luke 23:43). Not tomorrow, not in a thousand years, but "to day." So death holds no terror for a child of God. It is simply a translation from a world of woe to a heaven of happiness.

But even a Christian, a saved person, needs to prepare for death. Someday he is to stand before the Judgment Seat of Christ. His works will be tried there. Some of us have little or nothing to show for our service to Christ. Other works, those done for our own glory, will not stand the test of the Judgment fires. They will be met at the gate with the words, "You can get into heaven all right because Jesus has made it possible, but there will be no reward for you, since you did nothing for Him."

Some of you are not working for the glory of God. You are spending your lives on the things that perish, the things that will die with the setting sun. You are working only to gain position, wealth and pleasure. At last you will come up empty-handed before the Christ who saved you. If this is the case, do you think you are ready to die? Are you ready to meet the Saviour if you have done nothing for Him? The time may be very short. Don't you think you had better get busy for Him?

Then remember that when death comes, you won't have any more time to win souls. You have lost loved ones. Do you want to die before you have done your best to win them to Jesus? Are the children lost? Are you doing anything about it? Will the circle be unbroken in the sweet by-and-by? Jesus said, "I must work the works of him that sent me, while it is day: the night cometh, when no man can work" (John 9:4).

2. *What happens to the lost sinner at death?* In Luke 16:22, 23 we read, "the rich man also died, and was buried; and in hell he lift up his eyes, being in torments."

Conscious torment comes at death for one who rejects Christ. The body goes to the grave, the soul to the place of suffering. Later the body is raised and joined with the soul. Then the sinner is cast into the lake of fire prepared for the devil and his angels and his full measure of suffering begins.

IV. Is There a Chance After Death?

The answer is an emphatic *"no."* Ecclesiastes 11:3 says, "In the place where the tree falleth, there shall it be." And as a man dieth so shall he be forever, saved or lost. There is no opportunity for repentance after death. No gospel is preached, no invitation is given, no mercy extended. After death there is nothing left for the unbeliever but judgment, damnation and suffering.

Abraham said to the man in hell, "Between us and you there is a great gulf fixed: so that they which would pass from hence to you cannot; neither can they pass to us, that would come from thence" (Luke 16:26). Believe me, God knows how to fix gulfs. He has put ninety-three million miles between us and the sun. The lost man in eternity will be on the wrong side of the gulf between heaven and hell. God pleads with you to come to Christ now. After death you won't have another chance.

V. What About Deathbed Repentance?

Are they genuine? They are like all others, some are genuine and some are not. One Monday morning I was leaving Jacksonville, Florida, where I served as pastor, to go to Miami for a revival meeting. A call came from the hospital for me to go to a room where a certain man was thought to be dying. He had often heard me preach. I hurried over to see him and as he lay there in the hospital he made a profession of faith in Christ. He also said, "If the Lord permits me to get well, I'll go all the way with Him." I went on away for my meeting in Miami. When I returned to Jacksonville I learned that the man was out of the hospital and back home. I went to see him and he repeated his promise to go all the way with the Lord. Soon he was back in our church services, where he made his public profession of faith and was baptized. He became a faithful Christian and church member.

About the same time I visited another man in the hospital and witnessed to him of Christ's saving grace. He told me that he would look after his soul's salvation when he re-

A *Rendezvous With Death* 111

covered. But he did nothing about it. Soon he was back in the hospital, desperately ill, and again he made his same promise. But he never came to church to carry out his promise and, so far as I know, he was never saved.

I am afraid that most deathbed repentances are born out of fear. I wouldn't run the risk if I were you. Come to Christ now and be sure.

VI. THE POSSIBILITY OF SUDDEN DEATH

More than one half of the deaths in America are sudden deaths. Automobile accidents, murders, suicides, war, heart attacks, all take their toll. Many of those who die this way have no time to cry out for mercy and to repent, so they go out to face God unprepared.

Yet there is no excuse for anyone to be lost today. We have churches on nearly every street, we have Bibles and Christian literature everywhere. The Gospel is preached in pulpits, on radio and television. Oh, man in America, you are without excuse. "He, that being oft reproved hardeneth his neck, shall suddenly be destroyed, and that without remedy" (Proverbs 29:1).

Sam Jones, the dynamic evangelist of yesteryear, was preaching in a tent in a certain place. A young man stood for a few minutes on the edge of the crowd and listened. Soon someone heard him say as he turned away, "To hell with all that stuff." He went down to the railroad and tried to swing up on a moving train. He missed his footing and fell under the train and was crushed to death. His opportunity had passed. Again I say, "Come to Jesus now."

VII. THE ONE WHO CONQUERED DEATH

The Lord Jesus Christ conquered death for you and me when He rose from Joseph's tomb. And because He lives we, too, shall live. Our bodies sleep in the grave until He comes in the air, but our souls go at death into His presence. So death should hold no fear for the Christian. Let it come, he can laugh at it. It simply means that he is being translated from a sinful world to his Heavenly Home, and that's the most wonderful thing that could happen to anyone.

For the Christian, death is not the crossing of chilly waters, not a battle with a monster, not the grip of a cold hand upon the throat, not an icy breath on the face. It is a sweet relief from care and sorrow. It is the end of sin and sadness, distress and disappointment. It is an entrance into the sweet presence of Jesus. Paul said, "For me to live is Christ, and to die is gain" (Philippians 1:21). If you have lived for Christ, death will be all gain and glory for you.

Well, what does death mean to you? Will it be the end of every opportunity or the beginning of bliss? Will you go up or down? Will it be heaven or hell for you? You have the power of choice. Which shall it be, Christ and heaven or sin and hell?

A little boy was playing in the sand by the ocean. He built a little city of sand, with houses and stores and churches in it. He did not notice that it was getting late. Soon the tide came in and washed his little city away. He began to run from the waves. His big brother saw his distress, reached down and pulled him to safety, took him in his arms and carried him home.

So we play upon the sands of time. We build our little playhouses, we spend our little lives for this world. We become so busy that we don't notice that death is coming. Then suddenly it comes and sweeps us away and all that we have built up over the years. But we are not to be terrified. Jesus our Elder Brother knows all about it. He reaches down, lifts us up in His arms and carries us up to the brightness of our Heavenly Father's house.

This can be your experience, only if you are trusting Christ as your Lord and Saviour.

12

THE MESSAGE OF THE EMPTY TOMB

Luke 24:1-12

This old world has seen some dark days. It was a dark day when sin entered the Garden of Eden, when our first parents sinned and brought death and sorrow into the world. It was a dark day when sin had grown so great that God condemned the world and destroyed most of the human race by a flood. It is a dark day when a plague takes thousands of lives. It is a dark day when a tornado or an earthquake brings many people down to death.

But the darkest day of all was when Christ was crucified. Cruel hands forced Him outside the city wall, where they nailed Him to a cross. He hung there from nine in the morning until three in the afternoon, while His heart broke for you and me. Even the sun refused to shine. Yes, that was the darkest day of all, the day when God's beloved Son met death because of man's sin.

I can see His body hanging limp upon the cross. It must be removed before sundown. So we see two friends coming out to Calvary. Nicodemus and Joseph of Arimathea took the body tenderly down from the cross and carried it to Joseph's new tomb, where they buried the Saviour of the world. Later a Roman seal was placed on the tomb and Roman soldiers were set to guard the place where He lay. Jesus is dead now. It's all over. He saved others, but He cannot save Himself. He performed mighty miracles for others, but now He lies there helpless in death. And His disciples go about the streets, weeping and saying, "It's all over now. He is dead."

But death cannot hold Him. A tomb of stone cannot imprison the mighty Christ. Friday night goes by, Saturday goes by, Sunday morning comes. In the early dawn some women who loved Him came to the tomb. To their great astonishment the stone which covered the mouth of the grave had been rolled away. Frightened beyond measure the women rushed into the tomb and found it empty. As they sorrowed and wondered suddenly two men stood by them in shining heavenly garments. "This is the place of the dead," they said. "You are looking for One who is alive. Jesus is not here. He is risen."

That is the greatest, grandest, gladdest message ever given to the world. Jesus is living! Death could not hold Him, the grave could not imprison Him, He is living. Well, His friends saw Him in His resurrected body many times during the next forty days. Then He ascended into heaven and He is there today. It's wonderful, but it's true. He lives! He lives! We do not worship a dead God, but One who conquered death and is alive forevermore.

I. The Proof of the Resurrection

1. *We know that Jesus was dead.* Some have said that He simply swooned and that He didn't die on the cross. We know this is not true. He hung there for six hours, then they pierced His side with a spear. Joseph handled His body and knew He was dead. His disciples went back to their old lives, they knew He was dead.

2. *His body was not stolen, as some claimed.* The Jews didn't steal it, though they wished that they could truthfully say that they did. The Sanhedrin would have given any amount of money to refute the resurrection. The chief priests and elders wished that they could produce His body. The soldiers came to them after the resurrection and asked, "What shall we say?" And the Jewish leaders said, "Here is money. Tell those who ask that the disciples stole His body while you were asleep, and we'll protect you." (See Matthew

The Message of the Empty Tomb

28.) Think of it! Such testimony would have been laughed out of any court on earth.

The disciples surely didn't steal His body, or they would not have come to the tomb looking for it. They would have known that the doctrine of the resurrection was false, if they had stolen the body.

3. *The next proof is that He appeared many times to many people.* He appeared to the women, to the eleven disciples, to the men on the road to Emmaus, in the Upper Room, on the mount of Ascension. His close friends had been with Him for over three years. They couldn't be fooled. After the resurrection Jesus was with them, off and on, for forty days. They knew He was alive. Paul said that He was "seen of above five hundred brethren." All of them would swear that this was Jesus.

4. *The change in the disciples' lives was another proof.* Before the resurrection they were always ready to run. They were afraid of death, afraid of the Jewish leaders, afraid of the mob. But look at them now. They had seen Jesus conquer death and they knew if He could do that He would never let them down. They felt the strange power of the resurrection in their own lives and went out to give their lives away, all but two of them becoming martyrs.

5. *His influence on the world is another proof.* No man has ever had the influence that Jesus had. It has been the influence that only a living God could have.

Look at His influence on individuals. Saul the murderer became Paul the minister. Simon the profane became Peter the preacher. Drunkards have become missionaries, sinners have become saints and servants. They rose up from their sin and lived lives of overcoming power. Why? Because they had Christ's resurrection power within. No man has ever changed lives as the risen Saviour has.

Then look at the effect of Jesus on the world's history. There have been times when men thought that civilization was tottering toward a fall. But behind the shadows stood the living Saviour, with the power to turn the course of the universe His way. Look at the hospitals, the children's homes, the homes for the aged and the helpless. These things did not exist before Christ. They exist now because of His mighty influence. A dead man could never have inspired the building of these things. This is the work of a man who lives forever.

Yes, there is every proof in the world that Jesus rose from the grave. Now for more than nineteen hundred years His nail-pierced hands have been laid upon men and nations the world over.

II. THE TEACHINGS OF THE RESURRECTION

1. *The resurrection teaches us that all the claims Christ made are true.* He made some of the most astounding claims ever made on this earth. Someone, in speaking of these claims, said, "Jesus is either the Son of God with power, or He is a mad man." Well, when Jesus rose from the grave in His own power, He proved that all He ever said was true.

First, He claimed to be God. He said, "I and my Father are one," and "he that hath seen me hath seen the Father" (John 10:30; 14:9). In His resurrection He proved that He was God, God come down to the earth in human form. No one else could have had such power over death and the grave.

Then, He claimed to be the fulfillment of prophecy. All the prophets of old spoke of His coming. They said that they would know the Messiah because He would have power over life and death. Jesus had that power. When He rose from the dead He proved that He was the fulfillment of prophecy.

Then, His resurrection proved the truth of all His teaching. He taught some strange and wonderful things. For instance, He said, "Tear down this temple, this body, and in three days I will build it up again." When He arose we know that all He said was truth. We would say that today a man would be called insane if he said, "Kill me and in three days I will come back to life again." But if he actually did come back from the region of death we would call him a supernatural man. So when Jesus rose from the grave we must say, "He was and is more than a man."

Think of all the other things He said. He said that He could save us from sin, be with us in strength every day and take us home to heaven when the shadows fall. And He can and will do all these things. If He can keep His promise to rise from the grave He can keep all the other promises He made.

2. *The resurrection teaches us that we have a living Saviour.* Go to the grave of Mohammed, of Confucius, of Buddha, and you are forced to say, "he is dead and here is where he lies buried." But go to the grave of Jesus and you can say with the angel, "He is not here, He is risen." Our religion is not based on a dead man, but upon a living God.

We need a living Saviour to help us bear life's burdens. A certain man's wife died, leaving a precious little girl behind. Her bed was right beside her father's bed. On the night after the funeral the brokenhearted man could not sleep. Looking up to heaven he said, "O God, I am trying to trust you, but it is as dark as midnight." Then he felt his little girl's hand reaching out to him as she said, "Daddy, it's so dark, but I know you love me even if it is dark, don't you?" He pulled the little thing over into his own bed, held her close and soon she was asleep. Then he looked up and said, "O God, it's as dark as midnight, but I know you love me and I'll trust You as my little girl trusts me." And God's wonderful peace filled his heart. Oh, what would we do in the hour of sorrow if we didn't have a Saviour to bear our burdens?

Then we need a living Saviour to intercede for us. Our family consisted of many boys, but only one girl. Of course, my father was partial to her. There were times when I had done wrong and I feared the wrath of my father, but my sister would intercede for me and beg my father not to punish me. And many times he would forgive me for her sake. I deserved the punishment, but he forgave me because of my sister's intercession.

You and I often sin against God. But we read in the Book that Christ is up there interceding for us. We know that God often lightens the punishment for His Son's sake. We can thank the Lord that Jesus ever lives to make intercession for us.

3. *The resurrection teaches us that death is not the end.* We are going to live on forever. Christ in His resurrection was the firstfruits, we shall follow (I Corinthians 15:20-23). A tree in summertime bears its first fruit, but there is more later on. So Christ's resurrection presages our resurrection.

A man followed a fox to a cave. He saw tracks going into the cave, but none coming out. He therefore concluded that the fox was still in the cave. As we follow Jesus to Joseph's tomb we see the steps leading into it. But there are steps leading out, also. We know that He lives and because He lives, we, too, shall live. Death is not the end.

Some years ago I made a tour through the Champion Fiber Company's large paper mill in Canton, North Carolina. From all the surrounding area they bring in dirty logs by the thousands to the mill. I saw these logs go into a great chopper — nasty and dirty they were. I followed this conglomeration from one process to another. As certain chemicals were added to this mass of matter it began to change. At the end of the line it came out as beautiful white paper.

In like manner our bodies may be buried in the earth. They are filled with sin and disease and soon become corrupt. But one glorious day, when Christ comes in the air, He will raise us up and change us into His own glorious likeness. "Because He lives, we, too shall live."

This means that we shall see our loved ones again. A certain man's mother lived with him and his family. Each night as she went upstairs to bed, she would stop at the landing on the stairs and say, "Good night, I'll see you in the morning." One night, as this man looked up at his mother she seemed unusually beautiful and her voice seemed unusually sweet. "Good night," she said, "I'll see you in the morning." The next morning they found her dead in her bed. His heart was broken, but he received comfort from remembering that the last thing she had said to him was, "Good night, I'll see you in the morning." Ah yes, our loved ones are going down the

The Message of the Empty Tomb

valley one by one, but that is not all. We shall see them in the morning with Jesus.

One afternoon I conducted a funeral service and the burial took place in a small country cemetery. One of the women present said to me, "Please come over here for a minute." We walked over to the grave of her husband, who had died a few months previous to that time. The tears flowed down her cheek as she said, "Oh, when I go home, it's so hard not to find him there." But bless God, because of Jesus she'll see him in the morning.

But the resurrection means something greater and better. It means that we shall see Jesus. That's the best part of all. He is the One who loved us and died for us and saved us and made heaven possible.

III. THE CALL OF THE RESURRECTION

1. *The resurrecion calls us out of sin.* Every Sunday is Easter to the born-again person. Every Sunday reminds us of His resurrection. Every day we are called upon to forsake sin and turn our backs upon it forever. Sin crucified Jesus but He came out as Victor. With His help we, too, can win the victory.

Simon Peter loved Jesus, but there came a time when he sinned greatly against the Saviour and His love. But because of one look from Jesus, Peter went out and wept bitterly over his sin. And when Jesus came forth from the grave Peter was changed into a new man. He left his sin, became a great preacher and gave his life away for His Master.

2. *The resurrection calls us into a life of love and service.* After Jesus rose from the dead He gave His followers a worldwide command. They were to go everywhere, proclaiming the good news of salvation through Him who had conquered death and the grave. We may not all preach, we may not all sail the seas and serve Him in some foreign land, but each in his own sphere can give Him his very best. The best of life and time and talents and money and influence belongs to Jesus Christ.

Am I speaking to one who is lost, one who has never had

a vital encounter with Christ as Saviour and Lord? Oh, how much you are missing! What a great day this would be for you if you would receive Him as your Saviour and confess Him as your Lord. All of time and eternity can be better for you, with Him as your Saviour.

Am I speaking to some backslider, someone who has grown cold and indifferent to Christ and His service? Oh, what a time to start over with Jesus! Do you have a grudge in your heart? Do you have cranky ways which hinder you from serving the Lord? Are you giving the best of your time and energy to the world? If so, now is the time to throw such a life overboard and start living for Jesus.

In the olden days, in a certain Scotch village, all the fires had gone out on every hearthstone. But on a high hill outside of the little village a house was found where the fire still burned brightly. Then from each home in the village a man came to this little house, lighted his bucket of peat and straw and carefully carried it home. Soon the fires were renewed on every hearthstone in the village.

Is your spiritual fire burning low today? Then come with me. Let us seek Christ the risen Saviour. Let us warm our love and renew our vows at His feet. Then let us go out and live for Him as never before.